I0046802

Physician Leadership Matters

The Importance of Understanding the Regulatory and Legal Aspects of Healthcare

Timothy E. Paterick, MD, JD, MBA

American Association for
PHYSICIAN
LEADERSHIP

Copyright © 2023 by **American Association for Physician Leadership®**
978-1-960762-05-4 Paperback
978-1-960762-06-1 eBook
Published by **American Association for Physician Leadership, Inc.**
PO Box 96503 | BMB 97493 | Washington, DC 20090-6503

Website: www.physicianleaders.org

All rights reserved. No part of this publication may be reproduced, stored in a
retrieval system, or transmitted in any form or by any means, electronic, mechanical,
photocopying, recording or otherwise, without prior written permission of the
American Association for Physician Leadership. Routine photocopying or electronic
distribution to others is a copyright violation.

AAPL books are available at special quantity discounts to use as premiums and sales
promotions, or for use in corporate training programs. For more information, please
write to Special Sales at journal@physicianleaders.org

This publication is designed to provide general information and is sold with the
understanding that neither the author nor the publisher is engaged in rendering
legal, accounting, ethical, or clinical advice. If legal or other expert advice is required,
the services of a competent professional person should be sought.

13   8 7 6 5 4 3 2 1

Copyedited, typeset, indexed, and printed in the United States of America

PUBLISHER
Nancy Collins

PRODUCTION MANAGER
Jennifer Weiss

DESIGN & LAYOUT
Carter Publishing Studio

COPYEDITOR
Pat George

Table of Contents

Dedications and Acknowledgements

To my lifelong teammates that make my life joyous: my mom, dad, brother — Joe, sister — Eileen, my brilliant and beautiful wife Barb, and my amazing and brilliant sons TJ and Zach.

I want to thank Nachiket Patel, MD, FACC, FACP, FSCAI, for his contribution to *Physician Leadership Matters: The Importance of Understanding the Regulatory and Legal Aspects of Healthcare.*

About the Author

Timothy E. Paterick MD, JD, MBA, and Master's in Physician Leadership and Management, is a cardiologist with a passion for preventive health measures, sports medicine, the law, and teaching residents and fellows medicine. While practicing full-time cardiology Paterick has written over one hundred peer reviewed articles in medical literature, has been an invited speaker across the country on medical and legal issues, and has authored three other books: *Invest in Yourself: A Cardiologist's Narrative for Heart Health, Health through Hope: Look in People's Eyes*; *Physician: Time to Invest in Yourself — Work-Life Balance, the Needs of the Patient, and Medical-Legal Risk Management*; and *Physicians and the Law: The Intersection of Medicine, Business, and Medical Malpractice*.

His continued study of medicine, law, business, and leadership/management has led to an understanding of how they intersect and impact practicing physicians.

Dr. Paterick played college basketball at the University of Wisconsin – Madison on scholarship. He then graduated from Rush medical school in Chicago, Illinois. After medical school he trained in internal medicine and cardiology at the Mayo Clinic in Rochester, Minnesota.

Dr. Paterick is a lifelong scholar-athlete. He was named first team All State in high school and to the top 24 high school basketball players in America his senior year in high school. At the University of Wisconsin, he was awarded the Ivy Williamson award for outstanding achievement in athletics and academics. After completing medical education at Rush Medical College and his medical training at the Mayo Clinic, Dr. Paterick completed his law degree at the University of Wisconsin followed by his

MBA at Edgewood College. He also completed a master's degree from UT – Southwestern in Physician Leadership and Management.

Dr. Paterick's passion is teaching medical residents, physician assistants, nurse practitioners and cardiology fellows and young basketball players. Many medical residents and cardiology fellows have achieved high levels of clinical expertise through his teaching and mentorship. Both his sons, having played Division 1 college basketball, exemplify his basketball-teaching prowess. They are highly successful professionals reifying his teaching/mentoring abilities. He attributes any success he has experienced in life to his wife and life-long best friend, Barb. Dr. Paterick can be reached at tpaterick@gmail.com.

Introduction

THE IMPORTANCE OF UNDERSTANDING THE REGULATORY AND LEGAL ASPECTS OF HEALTHCARE

Many physicians are uncomfortable navigating the legal and regulatory requirements that loom over them in healthcare today, in part because this body of knowledge is not a component of a physician's educational background. Yet when the need arises, physicians should have a basic working knowledge of healthcare law and regulatory requirements. We offer some basic knowledge here.

Legislative bodies at the federal, state, and local levels pass laws that are codified as statutes. Statutes are elaborated into rules as interpreted by the administrative agencies assigned to implement the law. It is in this interpretation that disagreements surface between the agencies, such as the US Department of Health and Human Services (HHS), and the individuals and institutions affected by the rules. In addition, laws and regulations constantly evolve, so physicians must be attentive to the changing legal and regulatory landscape.

Healthcare is a highly regulated industry, especially regarding billing, compliance, human resources, licensure, liability, and fraud and abuse. Because healthcare is regulated at the state level, physicians should stay informed about any changes being considered in their state legislative bodies.

How does a physician attain the necessary skill set to manage a practice in the present legal and regulatory environment? A starting point is to review the organization's medical staff bylaws, rules, and regulations. They set the framework for the behavior the institution expects from its medical staff which, in turn, is critical for complying with federal and state regulations that apply to hospitals and clinics.

Most physicians cannot know all the intricacies of the legal and regulatory environment. Partnering with appropriate legal counsel and regulatory experts at the institution's disposal is critical. It is also important for physicians to stay educated on evolving key legal and regulatory issues.

Healthcare law is divided into specific areas, including malpractice, finance and reimbursement, regulations, credentialing and privileging of physicians, peer review, contracting, and fraud and abuse. Because each area is complex, many hospitals and healthcare systems contract with law firms that specialize in healthcare law.

On the regulatory side, healthcare organizations must comply with a wide variety of rules that range from local ordinances to federal Medicare billing. Physicians should be certain that internal organizational subject matter experts are in place to ensure the organization meets regulatory requirements relating to the medical staff.

HIPAA

The Health Insurance Portability and Accountability Act of 1996 (HIPAA) is a federal law that requires national standards to protect sensitive patient health information from being disclosed. HIPAA and data breaches are difficult areas for physicians to navigate. HHS estimates that approximately 25% of data breaches occurred with the theft of laptops. Mobile devices with patient or institutional data should have robust encryption capacity, and the medical staff should be educated and trained to appreciate the risks of physically removing devices from the institution.

KICKBACK STATUTES

Physicians involved in financial relationships within the industrial medical complex must understand the kickback statutes that often govern these financial relationships. Hospitals and health systems must ensure financial relationships are not rewards for physician referrals to the institution. These laws are similar to the Stark Law prohibition against self-referral. Some healthcare institutions have run afoul of the law by providing free services to a physician practice.

To meet the spirit and agenda of the law, payment to physicians must meet a fair-market valuation test and be reasonable compared to the local marketplace. Under Stark Law, physicians may not refer patients to entities in which they have a financial interest. Physicians should also be aware of the peril of arrangements in which they are hired as medical directors of health systems. The hiring entity must be able to show that the medical director activity provides direct services and there is a record of the time spent in the directorship role.

There are a number of exceptions built into the Stark Law that allow physicians and healthcare institutions some flexibility in developing financial relationships with physicians and in how physicians may legally refer patients. Antitrust laws through the Sherman Act prohibit anticompetitive behavior such as restraint of trade. The complexity of the financial relationships and these laws make it prudent for physicians to have all financial relationships reviewed by expert legal counsel.

IT'S ALL ABOUT THE MONEY

Intertwined with all the complex financial relationships between physicians and institutions are the fraud and abuse laws, the Medicare Anti-Kickback Statute, Office of Inspector General Administrative Civil Monetary Penalty Authority, and assorted state laws that are concerned with the effect of compensation based upon referral decisions of physicians. The fraud and abuse laws are concerned with several types of remuneration: remuneration aimed at affecting referral decisions made by physicians, remuneration to physicians intended to reward them for withholding medical care, and remuneration to a beneficiary intended to affect the choice of the beneficiary.

Physicians should only receive fair-market value for their services and remember that an organization should not attempt to buy physician loyalty. Fair-market value is defined as the value that is commercially reasonable. The amount of remuneration cannot be based on the volume or value of the referral to the entity, and the entity can pay the physician on a per-service or per-use basis. Fair-market value should be well-documented and preferably benchmarked against known and accepted standards.

Another important legal area physicians must understand is how recover audit contractors relate to financial audits. These private contractors are hired by the federal government to review payment histories in an effort to fix federal overpayments and underpayments. Physicians should work with financial teams to ensure appropriate charges are being assigned for services rendered.

EXPLORING A COMPLEX WORLD

Needless to say, there are numerous legal and regulatory hazards that physicians would be prudent to understand. We will explore in depth throughout the book many of these complex issues that physicians face on a daily basis.

Some physicians enter into private practice by default, and others by choice. All of us entered private practice medicine in a naïve mental state and departed with the awareness that we had not anticipated the financial incentives dominating private practice medicine, the perverse behaviors occurring in peer review, and the landmines within the federal, state, and local laws and regulations. Our "enlightenment and awareness" were the budding incubation and impetus of this writing.

We will explore our expedition in private practice medicine that made us aware of the shortcomings of the local, state, and national surveillance systems monitoring private practice medicine; the complexity of federal, state, and local laws and regulations; and the sword and shield present in many peer-review processes.

We will discuss important topics that physicians must know to meet federal regulations to prevent waste, abuse, and fraud and the moral and ethical responsibilities of physicians when engaged in peer review.

Each section will start with the rules and laws that apply to physicians in medical practice. The sections will include compliance issues for medical practices, peer review issues, and practice patterns across some areas of medical practice that do not meet the fiduciary duty of every practicing physician.

The ultimate goal of the book is to create an awareness of the aberrations of medicine that we observed and to argue for new local, state, and national policies and methodologies to oversee these practice patterns (measure what matters). We also hope to prevent future deviations from the law and the potential harm to patients and repercussions to physicians that result. Just as climate change is an existential threat to human survival, many medical private practice patterns are an existential threat to our society's health and financial well-being.

We hope this book will surface the issues society must address for the future of medicine to be patient-centered. This writing is inspired by and in honor of activists Ralph Nader and Lawrence Lessig.

SECTION 1

Compliance Issues for Practicing Physicians

This section outlines the rules, regulations, and legislation every practicing physician should know (Chapters 1–3) and then details aberrations identified in the private practice (Chapter 4).

CHAPTER 1

An Overview of Healthcare Enforcement Laws and Federal Healthcare Employment Laws

Federal regulatory policies directly affect how physicians practice medicine; transgression of these laws can lead to loss of license, exclusion from CMS payments, fines, and civil and criminal penalties. Breach of federal employment laws can result in similar devastating penalties. This chapter provides readers with a basic knowledge of these complex laws. It is an introduction to these complex topics and should not be considered legal advice or a comprehensive review of the regulatory policies.

All healthcare organizations must comply with an increasingly regulatory environment that directly impacts the medical practice of physicians. An understanding of mandatory federal regulations and employment law facilitates the development of compliance programs that prevent physicians from engaging in fraud, waste, abuse, and discrimination.

FEDERAL HEALTHCARE ENFORCEMENT

Federal laws define what constitutes fraud, waste, and abuse, and the penalties imposed upon physicians for transgressing these laws. The foundation of these federal regulation policies is the misuse of federal healthcare programs like Medicare and Medicaid, such as submitting excess charges, billing for services not rendered, or ordering unwarranted tests. These abuses increase the financial strain on the federal programs that are a government safety net for the elderly, poor, and disabled.

An example will illuminate the extent of this financial strain: In 2014, $600 billion of payment flowed into Medicare against $613 billion in costs. Simple accounting reveals a $13 billion deficit. Of the $600 billion, how much was paid by payroll taxes? The answer is $228 billion.

Doing back-of-the-envelope simple math leaves Uncle Sam with a vast financial strain.

Let's drill down on the critical concepts of fraud, waste, and abuse in medical practice.

Fraud is defined as an intentional act of deception, misrepresentation, or concealment to gain something of value. This implies a physician has knowingly made a false claim to obtain a federal healthcare payment. Examples of fraud include billing for services not rendered, billing services at an inflated rate, soliciting a bribe or rebate, and violating physician self-referral laws.

Waste is defined as using or expanding resources carelessly for no purpose. In the healthcare arena, waste is manifest when a physician uses resources without purpose or fails to control costs, and then passes those fees on to the Centers for Medicare and Medicaid Services (CMS) for payment.

Examples of waste include providing medical services that are not medically necessary and performing tests and procedures that are not clinically congruent with the prevailing standard of care. Waste is generally not intentional, but it can be. Regardless, overbilling CMS still carries consequences.

Abuse includes intentional or unintentional practices that directly or indirectly result in unnecessary costs to CMS. Examples of abuse include overcharging for services or supplies, providing unnecessary services that do not comport with the prevailing standard of care, and miscoding on a claim.

FEDERAL FRAUD AND ABUSE LAWS

The Office of Inspector General (OIG), CMS, and Department of Justice (DOJ) collaborate to address fraudulent and abusive practices in federal healthcare programs. There are five major federal fraud and abuse laws that practicing physicians should understand. Transgressing these laws may lead to loss of a medical license, exclusion from federal healthcare programs, civil fines, and criminal penalties. The laws are the federal Anti-Kickback Statute, the Stark Law, the False Claims Act, the Exclusion Statute, and the Civil Monetary Penalties Law.

The **Anti-Kickback Statute (AKS)** (42 U.S.C. § 1320a-7b) is a broad statute that prohibits physicians from intentionally offering, soliciting, or receiving anything of value to prompt referrals for services payable by CMS. Succinctly stated: It is illegal to pay or get paid for referrals that are covered by CMS.

The **Stark Law** is a strict liability statute that prohibits physicians from referring a CMS patient for health services where the referring physician has a financial relationship with another physician or a member of their immediate family.

The law defines financial relationship by compensation agreements and ownership/investment interests. Physicians who violate the law are subject to fines, repayment of claims, and exclusion from CMS programs. Whereas the Stark Law is only concerned with referrals from physicians, the Anti-Kickback Statute applies to referrals from anyone.

The **False Claims Act (FCA)** (31 U.S. Code §§ 3729-3733) is designed to protect the government from being overcharged. It prohibits physicians from knowingly making a false claim to CMS. "Knowingly" is defined as having actual knowledge that a claim is false, or acting with reckless disregard to the veracity of the claim. Penalties include civil and criminal fines.

The **Exclusion Statute** (42 U.S. Code § 1320a–7) is a section of the Social Security Act that explains why physicians can be excluded from participating in CMS programs and for how long. An excluded physician is forbidden from receiving payment from CMS for the duration of the exclusion period.

The OIG is mandated to prohibit physicians from participating in all healthcare programs for a minimum of five years if they have been convicted of CMS fraud; patient abuse/neglect; felony convictions of unlawful manufacture, distribution, prescription, or dispensing of controlled substance; and felony conviction related to fraud, theft, embezzlement, and breach of fiduciary duty, or other financial misconduct connected to the delivery of healthcare services.

The OIG has discretion to exclude physicians who lose a state license, are found guilty of failing to pay student loans, and/or are convicted of misdemeanors.

The Civil Monetary Penalties Law (CMPL) (42 U.S. Code § 1320a–7) authorizes the OIG to impose civil monetary penalties and program exclusions against any physician found guilty of fraudulent claims for CMS payment. Federal agencies impose penalties according to the Federal Sentencing Guidelines. Mitigating factors such as an effective compliance program, self-reporting, cooperation with investigators, and acceptance of responsibility can reduce these penalties.

The OIG recommends a seven-component compliance program that can reduce these penalties. The program entails conducting internal monitoring and auditing, developing compliance and practice standards, employing a compliance officer, providing education and training for staff, having in place a response to detected offenses and corrective actions, having open lines of communication, and enforcing disciplinary standards.

FEDERAL EMPLOYMENT LAW

Federal employment law bans employee discrimination in recruiting, hiring, job evaluation, promotion policies, compensation, and disciplinary actions. The law prohibits all employers from discriminating against employees or prospective employees who fall into the protective class categories, including age, gender, race, color, religion, sexual orientation, genetic profile, and disabilities.

The majority of physicians today are employees of a health system. As such, they are protected from negative treatment in the terms, conditions, and privileges in all areas of employment. This includes hiring, firing, discipline, pay and benefits, promotions and demotions, work assignments, training, harassment, and retaliation.

Healthcare employers that are subject to federal anti-discrimination laws are required to have a workplace free of discrimination, harassment, and retaliation. In the case of direct discrimination, an individual of a protected class is treated differently than a similarly situated employee.

Indirect discrimination refers to a policy or action that appears to be neutral, but in fact has an adverse impact on a protected class.

Employers are liable if the discrimination was a tangible employment action carried out by a supervisor, such as firing, demotion, undesirable work assignment, or benefits and compensation decisions. An employer may be liable for discrimination even if there is no tangible employment action. An employer may be liable if they knew, or should have known, about harassment or retaliation and did not take prompt and appropriate action to correct the behavior.

Important anti-discrimination laws that physicians should familiarize themselves with are Title V11 of the Civil Rights Act, the Pregnancy Discrimination Act, the Age Discrimination in Employment Act, the Genetic Information Nondiscrimination Act, the Americans with Disabilities Act, and the Family Medical Leave Act.

- **Title V11** applies to employers that have at least 15 employees. The law prohibits discrimination against protected classes according to race, color, religion, national origin, and sex.
- The **Pregnancy Discrimination Act** amended Title V11 to expand the scope of the protected class to include pregnant women. The act prohibits sex-based discrimination based on pregnancy, childbirth, and breastfeeding.
- The **Age Discrimination in Employment Act (ADEA)** applies to employers with at least 20 employees. It prohibits discrimination against applicants and employees 40 years of age and older. This applies to employee benefits, pensions, and retirement benefits.
- **The Genetic Information Nondiscrimination Act (GINA)** applies to employers with at least 15 employees and prohibits discrimination based on genetic information. Employers cannot request, purchase, or consider genetic information about employees, applicants, or family members.
- The **Americans with Disabilities Act (ADA)** applies to employers with a minimum of 15 employees. It prohibits discrimination against individuals with a physical or mental disability, employees with a record of a disability, and those perceived as having a disability.

- The **Family Medical Leave Act (FMLA)** applies to employers with at least 50 employees. The act entitles employees who have worked for at least 12 months and at least 1,250 hours over the past 12 months to 12 weeks of unpaid job-protected leave for specified family and medical reasons, such as birth or adoption of a child; care for a spouse, child, or parent who has serious health conditions; or serious health conditions that make the employee unable to perform their job.

CONCLUSION

Physicians would be well-served by becoming familiar with federal regulation policies and federal employment law introduced here. Violation of these regulatory policies and employment laws may have a significant impact on physicians' medical practice life, including loss of license to practice medicine, reputational damage, and civil and criminal penalties.

CHAPTER 2

The Importance of Understanding HIPAA Privacy Rule

The Health Insurance Portability and Accountability Act (HIPAA) has a significant impact on physicians' daily medical practice. Exploration of the privacy rule reveals a dynamic and evolving relationship between physicians, healthcare entities, and patients. Physicians must understand this relationship to maintain patient privacy, provide optimal medical care, and prevent potential sanctions for violation.

HIPAA is complicated, granular in detail, and broad in its administrative bandwidth. Transgression of the enumerated mandates of HIPAA can lead to loss of license, civil and criminal fines, and imprisonment. Becoming familiar with this complex law is a marathon every physician should run.

OVERVIEW OF THE HIPAA PRIVACY RULE

The HIPAA Privacy Rule requires physicians to implement policies and procedures that protect the privacy of patients' personal health information (PHI) and regulates how physicians use and disclose PHI with and without patient authorization. The Privacy Rule was intended to provide patients with rights over their health information, such as the right to examine and obtain their health records, authorize transmission of their PHI in an electronic health record, and request corrections to their PHI.

The Privacy Rule succinctly stated was meant to give patients more control over PHI, set boundaries on the use and release of PHI, establish safeguards that physicians must apply to protect PHI, hold violators of HIPAA accountable, and strike a balance when there is a public need for disclosure of PHI.

Entities the Privacy Rule Applies To

HIPAA applies to what are called covered entities (CEs). CEs include but are not limited to health plans, healthcare clearinghouses, and physicians who perform standard electronic transactions. Third parties that have access to patient information, called business associates (BAs), must also comply with HIPAA.

A **health plan** is an individual or group plan that pays for medical care. The law identifies a variety of organizations and government programs as health plans, including insurance companies, the Centers for Medicare & Medicaid Services (CMS), the Children's Health Insurance Program (CHIP), the Civilian Health and Medical Program of the Uniformed Services (CHAMPUS), and prescription drug programs.

A **healthcare clearinghouse** includes a billing service, community health management information system, or community health information system.

Healthcare providers are individuals or organizations that bill or are paid for medical services as part of their business.

Affiliated CEs are legally separate entities that are under common ownership. An example is an integrated delivery network that includes hospitals, medical groups, and long-term care facilities.

A **BA** is a person or entity that is not part of the CE's staff, but performs activities on behalf of the CE that include the use or disclosure of PHI. BA activities include but are not limited to claims processing or administration, data analysis processing or administration, utilization review, quality assurance, benefits management, and practice management.

When a CE recognizes it has a business relationship that meets the definition of a BA, the CE is responsible for guaranteeing that the BA complies with HIPAA rules. This is accomplished with a contract between the CE and the BA known as a business associate agreement (BAA). The BAA specifies each party's duties with regard to the PHI.

There are exceptions to the BA standard. HIPAA does not demand CEs have a BAA in place before PHI can be disclosed to a physician for treatment. For example, a hospital does not need a BAA with a specialist to whom it refers a patient. A physician does not need a BAA with a medical laboratory in order to disclose PHI to treat a patient. There are many more exceptions, and navigating the relationships can be intimidating. Physicians should seek legal advice when they are uncertain about the nature of a relationship.

DEFINITION OF PERSONAL HEALTH INFORMATION

Personal health information (PHI) is defined as individually identifiable health information held or transmitted by a CE or BA on paper, electronically, or orally, that identifies the patient and relates a patient's present or past physical or mental health condition, or identifies healthcare provided to the patient through present or past payments for treatment.

Types of PHI include identification of the individual associated with health information through name, address, telephone number, fax number, email, date of birth, date of death, hospital admission and discharge, license number, and other identifiers. Any of these data could be used to identify someone and link them to a PHI.

What Is De-identified PHI?

De-identified patient data is information that cannot be used to connect an individual to PHI. HIPAA does not apply to de-identified health information. It is a valuable asset to the healthcare community because it can be used to improve medical care, estimate the costs of medical care, and support public health initiatives.

Designating a Personal Representative

Patients have the right to select someone to act on their behalf regarding PHI. This personal representative (PR) has the same rights as the patient concerning the patient's PHI. The PR may have broad authority to act on the patient's behalf, or the authority may be limited at the patient's request. The CE and BA must observe the limits set by the patient. The CE and BA should review state law to identify regulations regarding the authority of PRs. HIPAA defers to state laws that expressly speak to a parent's right to access children's PHI.

If a CE has reason to believe a patient is the victim of domestic violence or neglect by the PR, the CE can choose not to legally recognize the PR.

Special Consideration of Mental Health Records

Mental health records are a subset of PHI that receive special consideration under HIPAA because they may contain personal notes and sensitive information that is not needed for medical treatment, payment, or healthcare operations. The mental health notes are kept separate from the rest of the patient's PHI and under HIPAA, are specifically excluded from the patient's general rights to access or inspect their own medical records. The CE must get authorization from a patient before psychotherapy notes can be disclosed to a third party.

The Uses of and Disclosures of PHI

Although HIPAA protects an individual's right to keep PHI private and confidential, there are valid reasons for physicians to use and share PHI, such as for communicating with insurance companies for payment and sharing PHI among physicians for patient medical care. There is a dynamic equilibrium between privacy/confidentiality and optimal information for quality medical care.

Authorization versus Consent

The Privacy Rule does not compel CEs to obtain patient authorization for medical treatment, payment, and healthcare operations. Patients may give written authorization or consent for use and disclosure of their PHI.

Patient authorization is an agreement that allows CEs to use and disclose PHI for purposes other than healthcare operations. CEs need authorization before using or disclosing PHI that is not allowed under the Privacy Rule. Relying on a patient's consent, when authorization is required, is an unauthorized use of PHI. An important distinction being consent does not equal authorization.

DISCLOSURE OF PHI

HIPAA permits CEs to use their professional ethics and best judgment when making a decision to share PHI without patient authorization in clearly defined situations.

Instances when CEs are permitted to disclose PHI include:

- Disclosure to the patient.
- Disclosure for medical treatment, payment, and healthcare operations.
- Patient permission to disclose.
- Use or disclosure for public benefit.
- Limited data set research.
- Public health purposes.

Instances when CEs are required to disclose PHI include:

- Patient asks for PHI.
- Patient asks for an accounting of disclosures.
- Disclosure is made to HHS for the purpose of compliance investigation, reviews, or an enforcement action.
- To protect the patient and the public.

The Minimum Necessary Standard as an Essential Protection

The intent of the Privacy Rule is to guarantee that any PHI accessed by staff or disclosed to another CE or BA is done in a manner that safeguards patient confidentiality. This is known as the minimum necessary standard (MNS) and is an essential protection.

CEs are mandated to limit use or disclosure of PHI to the MNS to accomplish the intended purpose. In light of the MNS, CEs determine which staff members need access to PHI based on staff responsibilities. There are exceptions to the MNS:

- Disclosure to a physician for medical treatment purposes.
- Authorization of use/disclosure by the patient.
- Use/disclosure required for HIPAA compliance.
- Requirement by HHS for enforcement purposes.
- Requirement by state law.

The Notice of Privacy Practices

A notice of privacy practices (NPP) is a statement by the CE that describes the procedure the CE has executed to keep PHI confidential and a description of how it will disclose PHI. It also explains how patients can access their information and exercise this right under HIPAA. CEs are required to write a NPP in plain and understandable language and make it available to all patients. A CE that has a direct doctor–patient relationship must provide a copy of the NPP on the patient's first visit and make a good faith effort to obtain written acknowledgment of receipt. Additionally, the CE should make its NPP available to anyone who requests it and post it in full view at the physical location and on its website.

The CE cannot compel the patient to sign the NPP and it cannot refuse treatment if the patient refuses to sign the NPP. Refusal to sign the NPP does not alter the CE's need to comply with the Privacy Rule. Staff should attempt to document why the patient refuses to sign the NPP.

PATIENT RIGHTS UNDER THE HIPAA PRIVACY RULE

HIPAA provides patients with a general right to access, inspect, and acquire a copy of their PHI for as long as a CE or BA maintains the information. Patients may request a summary, or explanation of PHI, and have the right to direct the CE to share a copy of this PHI with a PR. A CE must comply with the request within 30 days. The CE can obtain a 30-day extension with written notice to the patient detailing the reason for the delay.

Patients have the right to specify how they would like the CE to communicate regarding their PHI and the right to request that the CE amend the PHI. If the CE agrees to amend the PHI, it must make an addendum to the medical record and communicate the amendment to all individuals who rely on the patient's PHI. The CEs must inform all parties involved about the amendments and those CEs and BAs must make the amendments to the information they have.

Patients also have the right to request an accounting of disclosures. These requests can be made orally or in writing. The CE should document the request on an authorization form. The accounting of disclosures must be kept with the PHI along with the request for accounting and the name of the person who provided the accounting. The CE must complete an accounting of disclosures within 60 days of the request. A 30-day extension is possible if the CE provides a written statement explaining the delay and the expected date the accounting will be completed.

The patient has a right to file a complaint if they believe the CE or BA has committed a Privacy Rule violation. The CE must develop and implement a procedure that patients can use to file the complaint.

Privacy Rule Administrative Requirements

The HIPAA Privacy Rule, through its rulings, mandates the CEs to develop a comprehensive blueprint to safeguard PHI and avoid prohibited uses and disclosures of PHI. Entities that do not develop and implement a comprehensive plan may be subject to significant fines, costly curative measures, and reputational damages. The Privacy Rule sketches out the following administrative requirements:

- Designated privacy official.
- Training program for privacy policies and procedures.
- Privacy rule guardrails and safeguards.
- Process for complaint filing.
- Sanction for privacy violations.
- Mitigation plan.
- No retaliation or waiver of rights toward complainants.
- Policies and procedures for PHI protection.
- Development of a management policy for PHI protection.

There is a dynamic balance between managing privacy and providing optimal medical care. Failure to understand these emanations of the Privacy Rule and ensuing Privacy Rule violations can result in sanctions that affect the physician's ability to practice medicine, including the potential for loss of license, civil and criminal fines, and imprisonment.

PRIVACY AND THE NEW TECHNOLOGY

The United States Department of Health and Human Services Office of Civil Rights (OCR), the organization that has jurisdiction over enforcement of HIPAA, released a bulletin in December 2022 addressing the use of website tracking technologies (https://www.hhs.gov/hipaa/for-professionals/privacy/guidance/hipaa-online-tracking/index.html).

The message of the bulletin was that "regulated entities are not permitted to use tracking technologies in a manner that could result in impermissible disclosure of Protected Health Information (PHI) to tracking technology vendors, or any other violations of the HIPAA Rules." The bulletin identified commonly used website technologies that OCR believes could result in the disclosure of identifiable patient information protected under HIPAA.

For example, disclosures of PHI to tracking technology vendors for marketing purposes, without proper release and authorization by patients, would constitute impermissible disclosures and would violate the HIPAA Privacy Rule.

In addition to violating HIPAA, the OCR identifies "a wide range of additional harms to the individual or others," such as creating the potential for "identity theft, financial loss, discrimination, stigma, mental anguish, or other serious negative consequences to the reputation, health, or physical safety of the individual or to others identified in the individual's PHI." According to OCR, these types of disclosures can "reveal incredibly sensitive information about an individual, including diagnoses, frequency of visits to a therapist, or other healthcare professionals, and where an individual seeks medical treatment."

The bulletin is relatively detailed in its description of the various tracking technologies being used today and provides an overview of how the HIPAA rules apply to the use of tracking technologies by HIPAA-covered entities.

Tracking Technologies Used by Healthcare Providers

Use of website tracking software enables healthcare providers to collect useful data about patients and others who visit their sites. Tracking technologies include cookies, web beacons or tracking pixels, session replay scripts, and fingerprinting scripts. These tracking mechanisms are often not apparent to the user.

Tracking technologies often involve the use of a script or code on a provider's website or mobile app that is used to gather information about users. Collected data can then be analyzed to gain insights into the online activities of patients and others who visit the provider's website. Often information gathered is used in beneficial ways and can help improve medical care and patient experience interacting with web portals.

Yet, information a healthcare provider obtains through tracking could also be misused if it were to get into the wrong hands. Patient data, particularly data found via the login area of a website, is often sensitive and includes information that could be used maliciously to promote misinformation, identity theft, stalking, and harassment.

Covered entities are required to maintain the security of their electronic access to information under HIPAA security rules. Unauthorized access constitutes a data breach and invokes regulatory requirements that must be taken in the event of a breach, such as investigation, patient notification, and notice to the OCR.

As long as the data stays in the hands of the healthcare provider and is properly secured, the risk of misuse is low. The problem arises when third parties have access to this information.

Special steps must be taken to protect this data when a healthcare provider contracts out its data tracking to a third party. Use of third-party vendors is not at all uncommon. Providers may not have the internal resources to build their own tracking technologies. Even if they could develop the tracking system on their own, the use of vendor-created tracking is usually more cost-efficient.

A third-party vendor of tracking solutions may have access to sensitive data such as an individual patient's medical record number, contact information, information about appointments and procedures, medical device identification information, and other information that pertains to the patient's health care and may identify the patient's identity in connection with that information. This information will generally be protected health information under HIPAA and is subject to HIPAA privacy and security rules.

STEPS TO ENSURE PORTAL SECURITY

Much of the sensitive patient data lies beneath authenticated patient portal sites. As a result, the security of these portal sites is critical in terms of compliance with HIPAA. The OCR bulletin lays out requirements that providers need to meet to properly secure their patient portal sites, including:

- Configuring user-authenticated webpages that include tracking technologies to allow such technologies to only use and disclose PHI in compliance with the HIPAA privacy rules.
- Ensuring electronic protected health information collected is protected and secured as required by the HIPAA security rules.
- Ensuring that any disclosures made to the vendor of tracking technologies are limited to the information necessary for performance of the vendor's contracted tasks.
- Ensuring vendors enter into valid business associate agreements with the provider. Vendors who create or operate tracking technologies for a healthcare provider are clearly "business associates," and the contractual relationship requires compliance with standards for business associates contained in HIPAA.
- Ensuring that protected health information is not available through unauthenticated portions of their websites. The exception where there could be access from unauthenticated pages might be the login and/or patient registration pages. However, if tracking technologies on a regulated entity's patient portal login page or registration page collects an individual's login information or registration information, that information is protected under HIPAA.

If information on unauthenticated portions of the website addresses specific symptoms or health conditions or permit a doctor search or appointment scheduling without entering credentials and accessing secure portions of the site, collected data could include HIPAA-protected information. It is possible that information could be collected and identified to a patient through IP tracking, e-mail address, or other data. If this data is tracked, even from the "public" unauthenticated portions of the website, the private information could make its way into the hands of the vendor of the tracking technology.

VULNERABILITIES OF THE MEDICAL RECORD

Because patient-protected health information (PHI) often resides in medical records, which are considered legal documents, it is important for physicians to understand the benefits and risks associated with the medical record.

What is the purpose of a medical record? The medical record is a way for physicians to accurately track information related to a patient's medical history. Medical records also document and track notes about the various encounters and interactions of physicians with patients.

Who owns the medical record? Ownership depends on geography. In 21 states, the provider owns the medical record. In 28 states, ownership of medical records is undecided. In one state, New Hampshire, the patient owns the medical record.

How long must a healthcare entity or physician practice retain the medical record? Generally speaking, it is prudent to retain the medical record for 10 years for adults, 28 years for pediatric patients, and five years after the date of a patient's death.

What are the rules surrounding patient access to their medical records? Healthcare entities have 30 days to turn over patient-requested medical records and the cost to transfer the files must be reasonable whether the medical record is paper or electronic.

What about when a third party wants access to patient medical records? Sharing with a third party requires a business associate agreement.

The general rule for divorced parents is that the parents have access to the child's medical records. There are exceptions, such as when a minor consents to their own medical care, a minor receives medical care at the court's discretion, parents agree to allow their child to speak confidentially with the physician, and when parental rights have been removed by the court.

When an attorney seeks a patient's medical record through subpoena or court order, the provider must turn over the medical record, but wait until the statutory time limit.

Similarly, it is mandatory to turn over the medical record for court-ordered warrants, custodial situations, and required by law if incapacitated victim of a crime. It is voluntary to turn over the medical record for a patient whose death was caused by criminal conduct and to avert a serious threat to health and safety.

If a patient demands you amend the medical record, ask for the request in writing and ask that it be specific. The patient request for medical record amendment should be entered into the medical record. The physician has 60 days to respond to the request.

Medical records can support physicians when it comes to treatment accuracy and deter accusations of negligence. However, legal issues related to medical records and PHI may arise.

Clear and concise documentation in a patient's medical record is critical to providing quality medical care and ensuring accuracy and mitigating against a patient complaint, alleged HIPAA violation, or negligence claim.

CHAPTER 3

An Overview of Legal and Regulatory Compliance

All medical practices need strong legal and regulatory compliance. Some of the laws that can cause civil and even criminal penalties if they're violated include:

- Health Insurance Portability and Accountability Act (HIPAA)
- Stark Law
- Anti-Kickback Statute
- False Claims Act
- Civil Monetary Penalties Law

The Patient Protection and Affordable Care Act of 2010 requires physicians to have a compliance plan in place for doctors who treat patients on Medicare or Medicaid.

In addition, medical practices must comply with Federal Trade Commission (FTC) rules that regulate how medical practices can be marketed online and offline. The Federal Drug Administration (FDA) regulates the medications that can be prescribed and how drugs and medical products can be developed. Experienced healthcare lawyers are skilled in FTC and FDA legal issues, as well as other legal issues that arise with their healthcare industry clients.

LEGAL, ETHICAL, AND COMPLIANCE ISSUES GOVERNING PHYSICIAN RELATIONSHIPS

Physicians need to understand the laws and regulations related to how they bill for services, work with insurance companies, submit claims to the government, and enter into business relationships. These are the basics of compliance and can be managed through an effective compliance program.

The Office of Inspector General (OIG) recommends that physician practices incorporate the following into their voluntary compliance plans:

- Conducting internal monitoring and auditing.
- Implementing compliance and practice standards.
- Designating a compliance officer or contact.
- Conducting appropriate training and education.
- Responding appropriately to detected offenses and developing corrective action.
- Developing open lines of communication.
- Enforcing disciplinary standards.

The OIG guidelines are voluntary, not mandatory, and are not all-inclusive. An experienced healthcare compliance lawyer can explain what steps a practice should implement. The focus on the OIG voluntary compliance recommendations is on federal healthcare programs. Many of the strategies apply to private payers too, although there are differences that should be considered.

BENEFITS OF A COMPLIANCE PROGRAM

The OIG believes that a provider's top priority is patient care. A quality compliance program helps the practice better serve the patient. In addition, a compliance program:

- Optimizes how claims are processed and paid.
- Minimizes billing errors.
- Reduces the odds that the OIG of the Centers for Medicare and Medicaid Services will conduct an audit.
- Meets requirements of the self-referral, Stark, fee-splitting, and anti-kickback statutes

Effective compliance programs indicate that the doctor is making a good faith effort to comply with relevant laws. These programs also send a message to employees that they have an ethical duty to come forward and report erroneous or fraudulent conduct so that it may be corrected.

The OIG assumes that most healthcare professionals are honestly trying to serve their patients and trying to submit legitimate claims. Honest mistakes should not result in civil, criminal, or administrative action, according to the OIG. The criminal standard is proof beyond a reasonable doubt.

The OIG's compliance plan for individual and small practices also asserts that doctors who return funds that were billed erroneously should also be protected, provided there was no knowledge or reckless disregard of the truth. The best course of action is to make every effort to ensure bills are submitted accurately.

AUDITING AND MONITORING

A good place for physician practices to begin their review is to examine previous claims that have been denied and claims that have been routinely bounced for overpayments.

The physician practice should begin its review of its billing practices by asking whether the current billing process is working. The initial audit/ review should focus on the claims submission audit process. This review analyzes specific coding, billing, and documentation requirements. At least two people, a billing person and a doctor or nurse, should participate in this review.

Benchmarks should be established so the practice can compare future reviews against the initial benchmark. The benchmark review should confirm that:

- Bills are being coded to accurately reflect the medical service being provided (and that the service matches what's in the documentation).
- The documentation is being done on time and correctly.
- The services are "reasonable and necessary."
- There are no undue incentives for billing for unneeded services.

The benchmark review should follow the billing process from the initial intake of patient information through the submission of the bill and the request for payment. The review should examine parts of the process that may be red-flagged for possible non-compliance.

The OIGs' recommendations for the baseline audit are to examine the claims and services that were submitted within a three-month period after the staff was trained and educated on proper procedures. This way, the medical practice can analyze what's working and what's not.

After the initial benchmark is established, annual audits should be conducted on a random set of records. The OIG recommends reviewing five or more medical records per federal payer (i.e., Medicare, Medicaid) or five to 10 medical records per physician.

If errors are detected during the review of the random samples, the practice should take immediate steps to remedy them. First, acknowledge the errors offer appropriate explanations to the federal payers. Second, create new policies so the errors aren't repeated.

STANDARDS AND PROCEDURES

Someone in the medical practice should evaluate the billing practices and highlight issues that need to be addressed. In short, the office practices should be discussed with a lawyer who can identify procedures already in place and recommend other standards that apply.

Policies should be in place for responding to known errors. The practice should create and circulate a written plan for how to respond to the identified risk areas. Medical practices should regularly update clinical forms.

Individual and small medical practices that work with any of the following entities should incorporate the standards of procedures of those entities into their own standards and procedures:

- Physician Practice Management Company
- Independent Practice Association
- Management Service Organization
- A third-party billing company

Healthcare governing boards can look to "Practical Guidance for Health Care Governing Boards on Compliance Oversight" from the US Department of Health and Human Services for advice in designing a compliance program. In general, the compliance program should address several areas of concern, including areas of risk.

REVIEW OF RISK AREAS

There should be an assessment of known risk areas. Common risk areas the OIG recommends medical practices focus on include:

Coding and billing risks. Coding and billing should be reviewed for the following:

- Billing for items or services not rendered or not provided as claimed.
- Submitting claims for equipment, medical supplies and services that are not reasonable and necessary.
- Double billing resulting in duplicate payment.
- Billing for non-covered services as if covered.
- Knowing misuse of provider identification numbers, which results in improper billing.
- Unbundling (billing for each component of the service instead of billing or using an all-inclusive code).
- Failing to properly use coding modifiers.
- Clustering.
- Up coding the level of service provided.

The medical practice should understand how to match these risks with current federal and state laws and regulations for billing and private insurer requirements. All billing should match the documentation so if questions arise, the documentation is ready to support the truth of the bill.

Particular attention should be paid to issues of appropriate diagnosis codes and individual Medicare Part B claims (including documentation guidelines for evaluation and management services).

Reasonable and necessary services risks. When doctors order imaging tests, screening tests, and diagnostic tests that they believe will help treat their patients, they must meet the federal definitions of what Medicare and Medicaid deem "reasonable and necessary." Bills to Medicare and Medicaid must meet those federal definitions.

The billing should be balanced with the doctor's understanding that sometimes denials by Medicare and Medicaid prompt payment by secondary/private insurers. The main key is that the documentation must support the need for the test.

The same risk analysis applies to reasonable and necessary treatments.

Documentation risks. Records should be complete, accurate, and documented in a timely manner. Proper documentation should support the billing code and the reasonableness and need for the service. Medical records should identify where the care was provided and by whom. Records should be legible; it helps to have the right software to input the medical information.

Records should include relevant patient history and examination results, health risk factors, prior test results, the diagnosis, and the plan of treatment. The documentation should also include the patient's progress, response to treatments, and any changes to the diagnosis or treatment. HCFA form 1500 is a common form that should be reviewed for accuracy and verification.

Improper inducements, kickbacks, and self-referrals risks. The federal and state governments are especially concerned about illegal referrals and kickbacks because they directly affect the type and quality of care the patient receives. In addition to increasing federal costs, improper remuneration means doctors are making decisions based on what's good for them and not their patient. Often, it means overusing certain services because of an improper arrangement.

The OIG specifically states that it is essential that the individual and small physician practices consult with an experienced healthcare compliance lawyer. Violations of Stark Law, the Anti-Kickback Statute, and state self-referrals laws can result in criminal and civil penalties. The OIG recommends extra caution when medical practices obtain referrals from or give referrals to:

- Hospitals, hospices, and nursing facilities.
- Durable medical equipment suppliers.
- Home health agencies.
- Manufacturers of pharmaceuticals.
- Pharmaceutical vendors.

In general, any referrals should be based on the fair market value of the services.

Improper inducements can include more than cash; they can include waiving deductibles or coinsurance without reviewing the financial need of the patient.

The OIG encourages practices to review the following relationships:

- Financial arrangements with outside entities.
- Joint ventures with entities that supply goods or services to the physician practice or its patients.
- Consulting contracts or medical directorships.
- Office and equipment leases with entities to which the physician refers.
- Any gift or gratuity of more than nominal value to or from those who may benefit from a physician practice's referral of federal healthcare program business.

RECORDS RETENTION PRACTICES

Part of any standards plan should be a review of how medical records, compliance plans and documentation, and business records will be retained. This retention should substantiate compliance efforts by way of records of any calls on inquiries to federal payers.

The OIG recommends:

- Specifying the time that records will be kept — generally a set number of years.
- Securing records against loss, corruption, and other damage.
- Determining how records will be handled if the practice is sold or closed.

The OIG has detailed voluntary compliance suggestions for individual doctors and small medical practices. These plans can help the practice reduce the risks that that the practice could be charged with criminal or civil violations. The OIG plans focus on policies and procedures that make the submission of medical bills to Medicare, Medicaid, and other federal agencies easier and more accurate. The plans are intended for the entire office, not just the individual doctors.

CHAPTER 4

Compliance Issues in Private Practice

This chapter is about "regulability." Regulability is the capacity of a governing body to regulate behavior within its proper reach. For our purposes, the governing body is the Office of Inspector General.

On balance, the federal government is attempting to find equilibrium between physician/organization protections and constraints. The transgression of federal law puts physicians and organizations at great financial risks and potential imprisonment.

We first must explain how physicians are paid before exploring when that reimbursement transgresses the threshold from legal to illegal.

Physician compensation is based on various factors which should be specified by the employer in a physician contract.

WHAT IS wRVU COMPENSATION?

The acronym wRVU refers to work relative value units. Here's how it works:

Every CPT code used for Medicare and Medicaid billing has a coordinating wRVU that is pre-determined based on the complexity of the procedure or patient visit. A physician receives a specific number of wRVUs for every patient examination or procedure they perform. Those wRVUs are multiplied by a conversion factor, which is a specific dollar amount. The more wRVUs the physician has, the more money they will earn.

wRVUs are determined by three components:

- The work of the physician.
- Expenses incurred by the hospital or practice.
- The cost of malpractice insurance premiums.

RVU compensation is the most common payment model. Physicians employed by hospital groups and health systems typically receive compensation according to wRVUs. In many cases, a physician's base salary requires them to meet a certain minimum of wRVUs, which makes it an important measure of physician productivity.

According to a recent study of wRVUs by specialty, the following physicians report the highest median wRVUs:

- Cardiovascular surgeons: 9,822
- Neurological surgeons: 9,333
- Radiologists: 8,862
- Ophthalmologists: 8,438
- Orthopedic surgeons: 8,009
- Urologists: 7,364
- Cardiologists: 7,336

The top three surveys to be aware of are:

- Sullivan Cotter Physician Compensation and Productivity Survey
- American Medical Group Association (AMGA) Medical Group Compensation and Financial Survey
- Medical Group Management Association (MGMA) Physician Compensation and Production Survey

THE BENEFITS OF A wRVU COMPENSATION MODEL

The wRVU compensation model affords different benefits for employers versus physicians. Here's how each party can benefit from this payment structure.

Benefits for Employers

Hospital groups and health systems pay their physicians using wRVUs because it creates transparency. wRVUs are standard. The conversion factor is standard. There is no flexibility to pay less or more to one doctor over another (at least not in terms of straight wRVU compensation). Employers are able to compensate outstanding physicians through bonuses and other methods of reward.

Most physician contracts require that a physician have a minimum number of wRVUs per month or per year and the physician work needs to include a certain amount of patient care. This encourages physicians to have a steady stream of patients.

This model also leads to a more sustainable and competitive group of physicians. Most physicians need to retain their patients and acquire new ones to meet their minimum amount of wRVUs, which causes them to compete for patients, keeping the hospital as busy as possible.

The wRVU compensation model is a value-based compensation system. Consequently, it encourages physicians to be more productive, which means doctors are likely to see more patients and perform more evaluations and procedures.

The other major benefit of this payment model is that it's an easy system for practice management to administer. It's essentially a flat-rate payment system that does not deviate. Conversion rates and wRVUs by CPT code are adjusted at the end of every year for the following year.

Benefits for Physicians

Physicians benefit from wRVU-based compensation as well. For example, wRVUs are not affected by the differential in insurance payments and the percentage of the bill the patient pays on their own.

Physicians are paid for their wRVUs based on codes submitted, not codes collected and paid for. They are paid whether or not the employer is able to collect payment from their patients.

wRVUs also benefit physicians who prefer to focus on patient satisfaction rather than billing and collecting. They are able to dedicate more time to practice and less time to administration.

DOWNSIDES OF THE wRVU COMPENSATION MODEL

There are also some downsides to the wRVU model. The pitfalls for employers are different from pitfalls for physicians, so let's take a look at each individually.

Pitfalls for Employers

wRVUs are just one part of a physician's compensation. Employers still need to encourage and support their physicians' professional development. Hospitals that don't offer any compensation other than wRVUs are likely to see their best physicians move on to new employers.

In some cases, wRVUs are paid on a sliding or graduated scale. This can benefit physicians but may be difficult for hospitals and health groups to administer.

Pitfalls for Physicians

In general, wRVUs offer more benefits for employers than for physicians. Although physicians working with an RVU model won't be able to do anything to change that, they should be aware of the downsides of wRVUs.

Physicians won't be paid for everything they do. One of the biggest downsides to wRVU payment is that the payment only applies to billing procedures that have a CPT code. For example, mentoring younger physicians and handling other tasks outside of patient care are not billable.

The competition can get ugly. In most hospitals, wRVUs create intense competition among physicians in the same field. Colleagues tend to compete with their peers rather than support them. This is especially the case if the hospital offers a sliding-scale payment model. With a graduated scale, physicians earn more per wRVU. Physicians are less likely to refer patients to other doctors and more likely to compete to gain new patients.

Physicians might feel like independent contractors. wRVUs reward the volume of care, not the quality of care. With the pressure to have as many wRVUs as possible, some physicians may be tempted to focus on quantity over quality. This attention to quantity may lead to spending less time with patients and ordering excessive testing to maximize financial gain. This doesn't benefit the physician in the long term, nor does it help the patient.

Bundled procedures cause physicians to earn less. One of the worst aspects of wRVUs is the fact that some procedures get bundled together or discounted. This is often the case in bilateral procedures, where the wRVU for the second side of the body is less than that for the first side of the body.

For example, a physician who performs breast surgery will earn 100% of the wRVU for the left side, but only 50% of the wRVU for the right side. Most physicians argue that they should earn the full 100% of the wRVU for each side, as one side doesn't require less effort than the other.

When multiple procedures are done at the same time, no less work or time is required on the part of the physician, yet the second WRVU is often reduced.

Anything that alters the standard wRVU is called a modifier. Modifiers may be attached to a physician's WRVUs if they are performing a repeat procedure, working with a co-surgeon on the same procedure, or performing more than one procedure at a time.

Physicians could be underpaid. Physicians should keep track of their wRVUs to ensure that they're being paid for them. This can be a tricky thing to do.

Certain specialties have a limited amount of CPT codes, while other specialties have dozens.

The best way to keep track of your wRVUs is to review your patient visits and procedures at the end of each day. Record all the codes you plan to bill for that day and check it against the record kept by your administration. Also, ensure your billing department is using the correct codes. If you find any discrepancies, you'll want to address the situation.

WHAT IF PHYSICIANS ARE OVERPAID?

Imagine a situation where an independent physician group is in a joint venture with a not-for-profit, integrated health system. The integrated health system pays the physicians' salaries at 50% of the Medical Group Management Association (MGMA) Physician Compensation, but the physicians' production, based on the wRVUs, is at 25% of the MGMA physician compensation range.

Does this arrangement reach the threshold for joint ventures with entities supplying goods or services to the physician practice beyond normal business practices? Now consider the possibility that the physicians being paid at 25% above their wRVU production refer their patients to the integrated healthcare system. Does this raise a Stark violation?

The Stark Law regulates self-referrals made by physicians. It is a strict liability statute; there does not need to be proof of intent to find a physician has violated the statute. A physician cannot refer a CMS patient for health services where there is a relationship with another physician group. The law defines financial relationship by compensation agreements and ownership/investment interests. Physicians who violate the law are subject to fines, repayment of claims, and exclusion from CMS programs.

Whereas the Stark Law is concerned only with referrals from physicians, the Anti-Kickback Statute applies to referrals from anyone. All medical practices need strong legal and regulatory compliance, especially in light of risks of kickbacks, and Stark violations. The OIG is often "blind" to illegal practices, as they cannot "see" through the corporate veil. These complex relationships need outside surveillance to report to the OIG and prevent these apparently illegal financial relationships.

The OIG often cannot get past the "corporate veil" of an organization when the physicians have a "dark code of ethics." This dark code of ethics occurs when financial desires override the ethical and moral DNA of the physicians and the organization.

SECTION 2

Peer Review — The Shield and the Sword

This section outlines the regulations, rules, and laws every physician practicing medicine should know in relationship to peer review (Chapters 5–7) and then details irregularities using the private practice as an example (Chapters 8, 9).

CHAPTER 5

Practical Aspects and Legal/ Ethical Issues of Peer Review

The hospital staff physicians and the hospital administration aspire for high-quality medical care and the assurance of patient safety. Unfortunately, when quality concerns surface there can be reasonable differences of opinion as to whether a physician's practice pattern met the accepted threshold of the standard of care. This difference of opinion can lead to conflict that fuels a physician review.

All physicians working in hospitals should become familiar with the hospital bylaws and regulations. The consequences of adverse outcomes when subject to peer review can destroy medical careers.

THE IMPORTANCE OF THE PEER REVIEW PROCESS

The peer review process is important for physicians to understand, but is one that few physicians comprehend at a granular level. The challenge for physicians is that many of the issues presented at peer review are cloaked in legal concepts about which physicians lack education, training, and familiarity. The hospital bylaws and regulations are complex, and it requires time and energy to become knowledgeable in their intent and application in the hospital setting.

In this chapter, we will explore a broad range of topics related to peer review, including the roles and duties of the medical staff and the hospital administration in relationship to peer review, the intricacies of the credentialing and privileging process, the prompts for and process of peer review, the role of medical staff leadership versus hospital administration, potential liability and the need for legal representation to ensure due process and more. This conversation is important for all physicians to develop a deep understanding of the peer review process and how it can affect their reputation, professional status, and livelihood.

THE ROLES AND DUTIES OF THE MEDICAL STAFF AND HOSPITAL ADMINISTRATION

The relationship between the medical staff and the hospital administration with regard to peer review is complex. This complexity stems from the variable relationships of hospital-employed versus independent contractor physicians with hospital administration and the emergence of corporate responsibility for quality of care and patient safety.

These variable relationships must maintain the trust that an honest and fair peer review process will be available for all medical practitioners. A breakdown in that trust can result in medical staff chaos.

The medical staff and hospital administration must work in harmony to employ a peer review process that gauges professional activities and conduct. Professional activities must meet the standard of care and physician behavior must meet the hospital code of conduct.

The hospital board expects physicians on the medical staff to define and monitor processes for physician credentialing, evaluation, peer review, and disciplinary actions. Because these are delicate and sensitive issues, they can be best addressed by an organized medical staff that has a trusting relationship with the hospital administration. Staff physicians need hospital administration to clarify the roles and responsibilities of the president of the medical staff, the chief of staff, and the qualified administrative officer. This interplay is crucial in the development of appropriate medical staff and hospital administration relationships and processes.

THE MEDICAL STAFF BYLAWS: EXPECTATIONS OF THE MEDICAL STAFF

Outlined below are expectations that practitioners should have of each other as members of the medical staff. These expectations reflect current medical staff bylaws, policies and procedures, and organizational policies reflecting the medical staff and hospital administration's values, culture, and vision. These expectations provide a guide for the medical staff in selecting measures of practitioner competency.

Patient Care. The medical staff is expected to provide patient care that is compassionate, appropriate, and effective for the promotion of health, prevention of illness, and treatment of disease. The goal is to provide effective patient care that meets or exceeds medical staff standard of care as defined by medical literature review, comparative outcome data, and the results of peer review data. Medical staff members should demonstrate caring and respectful behaviors when interacting with patients and their families and counsel and educate patients and their families.

Medical Knowledge. The medical staff is expected to use evidence-based guidelines when available, as recommended by the appropriate specialty, in selecting the most effective approach to diagnosis and treatment. Physicians must maintain ongoing medical education, board certification, and demonstrate superior medical knowledge and technical skills.

Interpersonal and Communication Skills. The medical staff is expected to communicate effectively with other practitioners, caregivers, patients, and families to ensure accurate transfer of information through oral and written policies established by hospital policy. Practitioners should request inpatient consultations in a clear succinct manner and should be practitioner-to-practitioner in urgent/emergent situations. The medical staff must maintain medical records consistent with the medical staff bylaws, rules, regulations, and policies. All medical staff members must work civilly and effectively with all members of the healthcare team.

Professionalism. Practitioners are expected to demonstrate behaviors that reflect a commitment to continuous professional development, ethical practice, an understanding and sensitivity to diversity, and responsible attitude toward patients, family, peers, and the public.

Medical staff must act in a professional manner at all times and adhere to the Medical Staff Code of Conduct. There must be a prompt response to all patients' needs; participation in emergency call rotations as outlined by the bylaws, rules, and regulations; adherence to ethical principles pertaining to patient information, informed consent, and adverse medical and surgical outcomes; and use of sensitivity and responsiveness to culture, age, gender, and disabilities of patients and staff.

Credentialing and Privileging. Credentialing is the process of verifying qualifications to ensure current competence to grant privileges.

Credentialing involves verification of education, training, experience, and licensure to provide services.

The companion piece to credentialing is privileging, which is the process of authorizing a licensed or certified healthcare practitioner's specific scope of patient care services. Privileging is performed in conjunction with an evaluation of an individual's clinical qualifications and/or performance.

Credentialing and privileging are fundamental to the medical staff peer review and to building a trustworthy and competent medical staff.

Hospitals are expected to initiate a review of physicians requesting hospital privileges. This review identifies that physicians have the necessary education and training to perform requested privileges. A second component of credentialing and privileging is review of physician practice pattern to ensure they have met the standard of care within the scope of the practitioner's practice. A third component of credentialing and privileging is assurance that the physician has behaved in a manner consistent with the hospital's code of conduct.

REPORTING TO NATIONAL PRACTITIONER DATA BANK

The National Practitioner Data Bank (NPDB) was created in 1986 under the Health Care Quality Improvement Act. The NPDB is a repository for reports of medical malpractice payments and certain adverse actions related to healthcare practitioners. The NPDB is intended to be an alert system to gather and disclose adverse information about physicians and other healthcare practitioners to restrict their ability to continue their medical practices without people knowing of their previous incompetence or unprofessional actions.

The information reported includes but is not limited to medical malpractice payment, licensure restrictions and clinical/hospital privilege restrictions related to professional competence and conduct, professional society membership actions related to professional competence and conduct, Drug Enforcement Administration (DEA) certification actions, and exclusions from participation in Medicare, Medicaid, and other federal healthcare programs.

Even though the NPDB itself does not provide a private cause of action, NPDB reports have an impact on practitioner careers and reputations. The impact of a report depends upon the underlying facts and how the report is worded. Entities that report practitioners improperly may face lawsuits from reported practitioners.

Failure to report to the NPDB when required by law has serious consequences. Any malpractice payer that fails to report medical malpractice payments is subject to a civil penalty. Any hospital or other healthcare entity that fails to report adverse actions has its name published in the Federal Register and loses its immunity from liability under Title IV with respect to professional review activities for a period of three years from the date of publication in the Federal Register. Additionally, the Secretary of Health and Human Services (HHS) publishes a public report that identifies those government agencies that have failed to report information on adverse actions as required.

What actions must be reported to the NPDB? Hospitals and other healthcare entities with formal peer review must report professional review actions based on reasons related to professional competence or conduct adversely affecting clinical privileges for a period longer than 30 days and voluntary surrender of privileges while under, or to avoid an investigation.

"Professional review action" is a peer review action that is based on the competence or professional conduct of an individual physician that adversely affects or could adversely affect the health or welfare of a patient or patients. In addition, hospitals may report clinical privilege actions taken against healthcare practitioners other than physicians if the practitioners' professional competence or conduct could adversely affect the health or welfare of a patient.

A more extensive discussion of the National Practitioner Data Bank is included in Chapter 7.

CONCLUSION

Peer review, hearing and appeals procedures, credentialing and privileging, and medical staff bylaws are all critical to fair and equitable treatment of physicians participating on medical staffs. Given the present competitive healthcare landscape, it is imperative all physicians take the time to understand the peer review process and to be knowledgeable about the concepts that are embedded in the interchange between the medical staff and the governance of the hospital board.

A fair and honest peer review process is in the best interest of all participants on the medical staff and for the patients. It is prudent to have legal counsel review the contractual relationship between the medical staff and the hospital executive committee to determine all safeguards are present to ensure a fair and equitable peer review process. All physicians on hospital staffs must be assured fair and equitable treatment when issues are presented to a peer review committee. Lack of knowledge or understanding of the bylaws and policies is never a defense when subjected to peer review.

CHAPTER 6

Legal and Ethical Issues and the Mandate for Physician Leadership

Many of the issues that surface at peer reviews are veiled in legal concepts and underpinnings for which physicians lack education, training, and familiarity. All physicians working in hospitals should take a leadership role in ensuring fair and equitable peer review.

Physicians are thrust into the world of peer review without the education and training in the legal and ethical principles that are inherent to a fair and trusted peer review process. Physicians must understand that the purpose of peer review is to evaluate professionally a colleague's work. In medicine, an honest and fair peer review process is the staple of an excellent medical staff.

During a peer review, the reviewing physicians must pursue all the relevant facts and determine their veracity. Typical allegations against physicians are practice patterns that do not meet the standard of care or behavioral patterns that do not meet the accepted behavioral standards of the hospital. A fair and equitable peer review process is essential for a hospital that wants high-quality medical care and a safeguard for patient safety.

Organized medicine employs the peer review process as a methodology to gauge professional activities and conduct. Physicians have an ethical and moral responsibility to each other and to patients to ensure all hospital practice patterns meet the standard of care. The peer review committee must allow physicians the right to exercise freedom in their medical judgment but ensure that the medical judgment is accepted and consistent with the national standards of care.

To be objective and fair, disciplinary hearings where a physician's reputation, professional status, or livelihood is at risk must include the following:

- A list of alleged wrongdoings.
- Adequate notice of the right to a hearing.
- The right to defend one's actions.
- Reviewing physicians who have a similar scope of practice as the physician under review.

All reviewing physicians must disclose any conflicts of interest and recuse themselves when conflicted for any reason. The hospital bylaws and administration must ensure safeguards that guarantee all physicians due process when enduring a peer review.

WHAT PROMPTS A PEER REVIEW?

Peer reviews may be instigated in US hospitals for several reasons.

1. To determine whether the physicians requesting hospital privileges have the necessary education and training to perform the requested privileges.
2. To investigate the allegation that a physician is practicing below the standard of care.
3. In response to a claim that a physician is acting outside the boundaries of normally accepted hospital behavior.
4. As a random selection of cases to improve the overall quality of patient care.
5. In response to adverse outcomes to determine the root causes of errors and develop processes to prevent future adverse events.

The lack of a standardized peer review process has allowed varying decisions for similar alleged wrongdoings. This lack of standardization is a major issue that must be confronted by physician leaders.

UNDERSTANDING THE PEER REVIEW PROCESS

The importance of a fair and equitable peer review process is never so self-evident as when a physician is the subject of one. The birth of peer review conceptually started with Ernest Amory Codman. He was an extraordinary surgeon at Massachusetts General Hospital whose true passion was the science of quality improvement. Codman believed that by prospectively tracking outcomes, we could learn from patient results and advance the field of medicine. He contributed to development of the concepts integral to present-day morbidity and mortality conferences and started the first national registry in American healthcare.

Codman described patient tracking in a publicly circulated pamphlet in 1914: "Every hospital should monitor every patient it treats long enough to determine whether the treatment has been successful, and then inquire 'if not, why not' with a review to identify root causes of failure with a view to preventing similar failures in the future."

The approach to peer review today developed in the early 1990s when the American College of Surgeons implemented peer review to define the standard of care requirements to be met by medical staff physicians. The peer review process today includes a peer review committee composed of staff physicians who report to a board of directors. The crucial decision-making authority is the board of directors after an examination of the peer review committee's judgment regarding the charged allegations. As envisioned by Codman, this peer review process is required by JCAHO for hospital accreditation.

THE POTENTIAL FOR A "SHAM" PEER REVIEW

Despite the noble purpose of peer review, in some instances, the process can take on a darker purpose. The personification of fraudulent peer review is illustrated in the case of Dr. Timothy Patrick. Patrick, a vascular surgeon, sued Columbia Memorial Hospital (CMH) after he was subjected to what was perceived to be a deceitful peer review for economic reasons.

Patrick had joined a group practice in Astoria, Oregon. After several years with the group, he elected to decline partnership and pursue his own practice in the same geographic region. His previous colleagues reported him to the hospital executive committee at CMH for peer review, asserting "irresponsible behavior" in his medical care of patients.

The peer review committee was chaired by a member of the group Patrick left to pursue his own practice. An investigation of the alleged "irresponsible behavior" was undertaken, and the committee voted to terminate Patrick's hospital privileges.

Patrick filed a federal antitrust lawsuit against the Astoria clinic physicians claiming the defendants partook in a bad faith peer review to quash competition. The United States Supreme Court ruled in favor of Patrick and awarded him $2.2 million (*Patrick v Burget*, 1988).

The Patrick decision had a huge negative impact on the necessary and important peer review process and affected physicians' willingness to participate in peer review. The response to this physician reticence was the federal Health Care Quality Improvement Act (HCQIA). This act provided physician immunity when participating in peer review subject to several factors, including:

- The purported allegation brought to the peer review committee was a furtherance of quality of care issues.
- There would be a due diligence approach to fact finding.
- There would be adequate notice and a fair hearing procedure offered to the physician under review.

The introduction of HCQIA transformed the law, granting peer review committees and hospitals limited immunity to almost unqualified immunity. This transformative Congressional ruling created a situation of grave trepidation for physicians working in a setting of intense marketplace competition where there are attempts by hospitals to stifle competition to have control of the marketplace.

Today, sham reviews still occur, and the courts are often viewed as kangaroo courts when considering interference of competition issues. Courts often view hospitals as virtuous entities that are solely interested in quality medical care and patient safety, and they assume that the hospital administration wants to uncover and address all medical errors and safety issues that occur in the hospital so they could be prevented in the future. This suggests a blind justice called the "rule of non-review," which implies that the governing board of a private entity, like a hospital, has the right to determine and direct its own internal business and medical affairs.

This type of public policy mandates that physician leaders engage in the peer review process to ensure that peer review is honest, fair, and equitable.

THE ESSENCE OF PEER REVIEW

Physicians in the United States accept peer review as an important safeguard to patient health and safety, but there is some distrust because of a lack of understanding of the legal underpinnings of the process. Health insurance companies have made a huge impact on the peer review process; they are now mandating evidence of quality peer review activity among the doctors in an institution prior to entering into an arrangement with the group of doctors or with the hospital.

The mission statement of the hospital often asserts that the institution aspires to a unified goal of transparency and partnership between the medical staff and the hospital administration to ensure equitable treatment of all disputes arising between a physician and the medical staff. Unfortunately, there are situations where the physician brought into the process and the medical staff have different opinions about the alleged practice pattern and whether it meets the accepted standard of care. The complexity for physicians is that many issues of a peer review are veiled in legal concepts in which physicians lack education, training, and familiarity.

The peer review process presents a varied range of issues that warrants legal knowledge and insights. It is imperative to have legal counsel when developing the foundation of the peer review process to ensure that ethical, legal, and accreditation principles are developed. Physician leadership must play a critical role in meeting this goal so physicians are assured of equity and fairness.

This approach is epitomized in an Arkansas statute that provides that medical staff can, as a matter of law, "engage independent legal counsel to review a professional review action before a final recommendation is made or final action taken." This is particularly important for physicians who are not hospital employees and may represent competition to the employed hospital physicians. All physicians deserve a fair and equitable hearing process and must have the ability to appeal any decisions that impact reputation, professional status, or livelihood.

HEARINGS AND APPEALS

The peer review process quickly identifies the polarity between the physician subject to peer review and the investigative group of physicians. A hearing officer is appointed to preside over the process and offer advice to the hearing committee. The peer review committee's decision can be appealed to the hospital board of directors, which makes the final decision or makes a recommendation to the peer review committee for the final decision.

It is problematic that hospital attorneys often represent the peer review committee and offer advice. The physician facing allegations may request that the peer review body use counsel not employed by the hospital or from a firm utilized by the hospital. This was highlighted in *Yaqub vs. Salinas Memorial Healthcare System*, in which the court warned that it would strain the due process clause to allow the hospital attorney, who took an active role in assisting the medical executive committee to bring charges against the appellant, to serve as an advisor to the board in the hearing. This type of judicial commentary is advocating for a true due process under the law, and it is crucial for physician leaders to understand this ruling.

MEDICAL STAFF BYLAWS

Generally, the recognized "majority view" is that medical staff bylaws are interpreted as a contract between the hospital and the medical staff. Even in those jurisdictions where the bylaws are not contractual in nature, differences in opinion between hospital and staff may lead to the need for a process allowing full hearings overseen by impartial judges. Thus, the hospital bylaws must allow active medical staff members to vote on their ability to participate in the elaboration of the rules and regulations impacting physicians, which only the hospital executive committee can act upon.

Therefore, it is incumbent upon the medical staff to hire independent counsel to review medical staff bylaws to ensure that they contain provisions that allow due process and equitable treatment of all staff members and to attain physician membership on the executive committee.

STANDARDIZATION OF PEER REVIEW

The need for standardization of the peer review process is epitomized in the Patrick case. Additional studies have demonstrated that peer reviews are often unreliable measures of quality and have not served the envisioned function of quality improvement.

Regulation of peer reviews should result in a two-fold effect: improvement in quality and decreased abuse of the process through sham reviews. National standardization efforts for peer reviews remain challenging, as the process is costly, time intensive, and requires extensive resources. Several models at diverse US hospitals have shown that standardization and structuring of the review process can improve medical care. Another approach is to develop additional protection of the peer review process involving external review to verify that the actions taken are in agreement with JACHO and HCQIA requirements.

CONCLUSION

Peer review, hearing and appeals procedures, credentialing and privileging, and medical staff bylaws are all critical to the fair and equitable treatment of physicians participating on medical staffs. Given the present healthcare landscape, it is imperative that all physicians take the time to understand the peer review process and to become knowledgeable in legal concepts that are embedded in the interchange between the medical staff and the governance of the hospital board.

A fair and honest peer review process is in the best interest of all participants on the medical staff and of the patients. Physician leaders must ensure all physicians on hospital staffs receive fair and equitable treatment when issues are presented to a peer review committee.

The intense competition for patients in the medical marketplace and the highly politicized US healthcare system has been of concern to physicians seeking a fair and equitable peer review process. The immunity granted to peer review committees through the HCQIA has the potential to have a devastating effect on a physician's professional status or livelihood.

Considering congressional and judicial tolerance of this quandary, substantial and meaningful physician leadership is necessary to remedy the potential deficiencies of the present-day peer review process. Furthermore, further research is needed to study the peer review process and its outcomes to determine if peer review reforms have altered the prevalence of sham reviews, improved the quality of care, and ensured patient safety.

CHAPTER 7

The National Practitioner Data Bank: Requisite Medical Legal Issues for Physicians

An understanding of the National Practitioner Data Bank will allow physicians to participate in peer review with a deeper understanding of the medical and legal issues they confront in relationship to hospital privileges and the NPDB. Reports to the NPDB can have a large impact on a physician's reputation, livelihood, and ability to practice medicine.

The National Practitioner Data Bank (NPDB) was established by the Health Care Quality Improvement Act (HCQIA) of 1986, as amended (42 U.S.C. 11101-et. seq.) The HCQIA authorizes the NPDB to collect reports of a wide variety of actions by local, state, and federal entities.

A broad spectrum of organizations have access to the NPDB data systems, including hospitals, healthcare facilities that have recognized peer review processes, and state medical boards. Medical malpractice payers, state medical boards, professional societies with formal peer review, and hospitals report information under HCQIA.

It is critical for physicians to understand the ins and outs of the NPDB as the playing field in medicine has changed dramatically since the introduction of corporate medicine. Playing the game of hospital medicine without knowledge of the game rules is like walking in quicksand.

NPDB REPORTING

The NPDB is a repository for reports of medical malpractice payments and certain adverse actions related to healthcare practitioners. The purpose of the NPDB is to be an alert system to collect and divulge unfavorable information about physicians to restrict their ability to continue their medical practice without patients knowing of their previous issues of competence or unprofessional actions.

What information is reported to the NPDB? Reportable data include medical malpractice payments, licensure restrictions related to professional fitness and conduct, clinical hospital privilege restrictions related to professional competence and conduct, DEA certification actions, and sanctions and exclusions related to participation in Medicare, Medicaid, and other federal healthcare programs are all reported to the NPDB.

Hospitals and other healthcare bodies with formal peer review must report professional review actions grounded upon "professional review action" that are related to professional competence or conduct negatively affecting clinical privileges for a period of longer than **30 days,** or when physicians relinquish privileges while under, or to circumvent an investigation.

"Professional review action" is a peer review action based on the competence or professional conduct of an individual physician that could negatively impact the medical care of a patient.

Why is it important for physicians to understand NPDB reporting requirements? Because reporting and not reporting to the NPDB can have serious consequences for a physician's career and reputation. The NPDB does not provide a private cause of action; entities that report practitioners improperly may face lawsuits from the reported practitioner for career/reputation damage and/or intentional infliction of emotion distress. The impact of the report depends upon the proximate and contiguous circumstances and the language used in the report. Alternatively, failing to report to the NPDB when required by law may have grave consequences.

The following are examples of when failing to report has serious repercussions:

- Any malpractice payer that does not report medical malpractice payments is subject to civil penalty for each payment not reported.
- Any hospital/healthcare entity that fails to report unfavorable actions will have its name published in the Federal Register and the healthcare entity will lose its immunity from liability under Title IV with respect to professional review for three years.

- Additionally, the Secretary of Health and Human Services (HHS) shall publish a public report of the government agencies that have failed to report information as required.

LEGAL REQUIREMENTS AND MECHANICS OF REPORTING PHYSICIANS

A Texas court identified that a physician's restriction to practice begins at the time the physician cannot practice the full scope of their practice.

Consider the case of Dr. Walker, a general surgeon holding medical staff privileges at a hospital in Lufkin, Texas. The hospital issued Walker a corrective action plan following a peer review evaluation of his medical care of patients.

The improvement plan mandated that Walker's surgical privileges be restricted until he performed five bowel surgeries with a proctor. The corrective action plan did not specify a time period for the requirements. After 30 days, Walker had not completed the five bowel surgeries and the hospital reported him to the NPDB. Walker sued the hospital seeking injunctive relief.

The court held the hospital erred because the corrective action failed to specify a time period. The court concluded, "whether a proctoring sanction is reportable should be established by the terms of the sanction at the time it is delivered, and not by whether, in fact, it takes more than 30 days to satisfy the requirement."

From the NPDB perspective, the report to the NPDB should be made if the restriction lasts for a period of time exceeding 30 days irrespective of the number of cases needed in the corrective action. The NPDB clarifies that an agreement not to exercise privileges during an investigation is a restriction of privileges. Any restriction of privileges while under investigation is considered a relinquishment of privileges and must be reported.

A practitioner cannot voluntarily agree to restrict privileges to avoid reporting. The 2018 Guidebook states that if a proctor is required for a physician to engage in clinical privileges for more than 30 days, it is reportable. Alternatively, if a proctor is not necessary, the action should not be reported.

Prior to 2018, it was unclear when the review process for reapplication became an investigation. The 2018 Guidebook answers the question by stating that this depends on whether "the reappointing hospital had specific concerns" about the applicant's competence. The NPDB Guidebook made it clear that follow-up questions do not necessarily create an investigation.

Resignation of an applicant prior to a final decision of an applicant's reappointment, where there are specific concerns about the applicant's competence, will be reportable.

Age Discrimination in Employment Act and The Americans with Disabilities Act

Fifty percent of the U.S. physician force is 50 years of age or older. There are no laws or rules regulating the competency assessment of aging physicians; aging has variable effects on people's cognitive and physical fitness capacity. This issue is fraught with complexity because colleagues may be reluctant to question the competence or skill of an aging physician because of long, respected careers and a reputation in the community.

In the employment context, assessing age- and health-related competency issues links two sets of laws: disability and age discrimination laws. Fair employment laws and the Age Discrimination in Employment Act (ADEA) attempt to prevent discrimination in employment based on age. The Americans with Disabilities Act (ADA) attempts to prevent discrimination against those with disabilities.

For decades, courts seemed to accept the notion of mandatory retirement ages if the mandate was linked to public safety. There are no case reports in which a court reviewed a healthcare employer's mandatory retirement age. In fact, courts would likely reject a mandatory retirement age for physicians. Instead, common practice is to use screening mechanisms for cognitive and physical fitness. The disability discrimination provisions of the ADA strive for case–specific, individualized assessment.

ADA and ADEA in the Medical Staff Context

The ADA and ADEA do not apply where a physician is a member of the medical staff. Hospitals have more autonomy to adopt age and cognitive/fitness-for-duty examinations in this context, including age-based competency testing.

Testing should have a nexus to the nature of the privileges. The physician being tested should have a detailed understanding of the necessary cognitive and physical skills for the specific specialty. For example, a radiologist needs good visual acuity and a surgeon needs goo manual dexterity and physical stamina.

In a case related to Title III of the ADA, which prohibits discrimination on the basis of disability in the activities of organizations generally open to the public, a court ruled in favor of Dr. Hertz, who was terminated from a hospital medical staff because of a disability. Hertz was disabled by bipolar disorder and sleep apnea. Aurora Medical Center brought a motion to dismiss the suit based on the argument that Title II only applied to the hospital's clients and visitors. The court found that a physician acting as an independent contractor may sue a hospital under ADA Title III for denial of staff privileges because the physician, like a patient, using the hospital for personal benefit and the good of the public. The message: Ensure that any fitness-for-duty testing is job-related and consistent with business necessity.

PEER REVIEW AND MEDICAL STAFF LITIGATION

A cardiologist was summarily suspended by the medical executive committee (MEC) for what the hospital considered substandard care provided to one of the cardiologist's patients. The peer review committee noted four peer review incidents and 10 anonymous reports (MIDAS) involving inadequate care or management as support for the suspension.

The hospital's medical staff bylaws stated that upon suspension, a physician is entitled to request an intra-professional conference that is required to occur within a defined period of time. The bylaws also provided that the physician would have the right to "inspect all pertinent and non-privileged information in the hospital's possession prior to the intra-professional conference."

The hospital granted the conference, but the physician alleged they did not give complete access to the records he requested. The hospital provided only four peer review records. The panel recommended that the hospital maintain the summary judgment.

The cardiologist sued for injunctive and declaratory relief. The Licensing Act of Illinois requires hospitals to include certain minimum procedures in their bylaws related to staff privilege decisions. The law includes a right to a fair hearing for administrative summary suspension. The court ruled the cardiologist had a right to inspect all applicable records to the intra-professional conference. The message: follow the complete process with issues related to medical staff privileges.

A second case addresses whether a physician has a property interest in medical staff privileges and whether a hospital violates its bylaws by using a summary suspension on a non-patient care case.

Dr. Chang was the chief medical officer (CMO) at the hospital. In March 2019, two hospital employees brought claims about Chang to human resources, alleging that Chang had sexually harassed them. The hospital hired an outside attorney to investigate the situation. Chang was placed on "restrictions and directives" pursuant to medical staff bylaws.

The attorney determined that Chang had engaged in unwelcome sexual activity toward the employees, including sexual intercourse, using coercion and intimidation. After the required process, Chang's medical privileges were summarily suspended.

Chang filed a complaint for declaratory and injunctive relief, citing violations of federal and state constitutional due process rights, federal and state law, and hospital bylaws. Chang requested the court to enjoin the hospital from reporting his suspension to the NPDB.

The court considered these critical issues:

- Did Chang have a property interest in his medical staff privileges that triggered constitutional due process protection? No.
- Did the hospital follow HCQIA due process requirements of a formal hearing before summarily suspending the physician? Yes.
- Does HCQIA require imminent danger to exist before a summary restraint is imposed? No.
- Does sexual harassment of an employee rise to the same level of wrongdoing as impairing patient safety? Yes.

The court found:

- The hospital had followed HCQIA's requirements and therefore denied an injunction.
- The suspension was proper and the hospital could report to the NPDB.
- The hospital did not violate hospital bylaws by issuing a summary suspension on a non-patient medical care case.

CONCLUSION

Knowledge of NPDB reporting procedures, what actions must be reported to the NPDB, the case law applicable to reporting to NPDB, the special issues facing aging physicians in light of the Age Discrimination in Employment Act (ADEA) and Americans with Disabilities Act (ADA), and the recent evolving peer review and medical staff litigation will help physicians participate effectively in peer review and will reduce the likelihood of a physician being a subject of NPDB reports.

CHAPTER 8

The "Shield" of Peer Review Observed in Private Practice

Hospitals attempt to find an equilibrium between physician protections and physician constraints. While modalities of constraint can be used as swords against individuals (Chapter 9), modalities of protection can be used as shields. This chapter outlines the unethical and illegal use of "the shield" by the hospital peer review group.

An element of credentialing and privileging is the assurance that the physician has behaved in a manner consistent with the hospital's code of conduct. This case involved a practicing cardiologist abridging the hospital code of ethics.

As stated previously, during a peer review, the reviewing physicians must pursue all the relevant facts and determine their veracity. Typical allegations against physicians are practice patterns that do not meet the standard of care, or behavioral patterns that do not meet the accepted moral/behavioral standards of the hospital. Medical staff members reviewing a colleague must proceed in a fair and honest manner. A fair and equitable peer review process is essential for a hospital that wants high-quality medical care and a safeguard for patient safety.

The relevant facts of this case defy the outcome of the peer review process. The practicing cardiologist was married with two children and a wife who was pregnant. It was common knowledge that the cardiologist was having "an affair" with a married sonographer who worked at the hospital. In fact, their sexual encounters were often on hospital property. The hospital physicians knew about the relationships and that the behavior abridged the moral and ethical code of the hospital bylaws, but they chose to look the other way.

The case was ultimately brought before the peer review committee, yet the peer review committee took no action. The determination should have been for the cardiologist to have his hospital privileges revoked and his case referred to the NPDB. The peer review committee was motivated by what others could not know: Knowledge and retraction of privileges would have impacted the group practice's financial bottom line. They made their moral and ethical duties invisible by looking the other way. The outrageous behavior of the cardiologist was ignored.

SHIELDS AND COVER UPS

This particular case represents a sham review, whereby a peer group shielded a physician from the normal peer review actions mandated by his egregious behavior. This type of "cover up" puts the hospital peer review group at legal risk. It also causes one to wonder what other types of "cover ups" were occurring. This peer review case exposes the immorality that can occur when medical groups are protecting their bottom line. But this also exposes the legal risk a hospital assumes with this irresponsible peer review action. The next chapter will introduce you to the malevolent face of this peer group: "the sword" of peer review.

CHAPTER 9

The "Sword" of Peer Review Observed in Private Practice

The two cases presented here are real-world experiences of cardiology and surgery physicians who experienced the agony of going before the medical executive committee and medical executives. It emphasizes the rogue nature of peer review and corporate medicine.

The peer review process was developed for the purpose of improving the quality of care for patients and ensuring patient safety. Good faith peer review should be collegial, just, and educational, and ensure due process. An unfortunate abuse of the medical peer review process is known as a "sham" or malicious peer review.

In an American Medical Association study in 2007, 15% of surveyed physicians indicated that they were aware of peer review misuse, but cases were difficult to prove in the difficult-to-navigate legal system. Factors that increase the risk of sham peer review include being a solo physician or part of a small group, being a new physician, or being in a high-risk specialty. The underlying theme in malicious peer review is often maintaining market share.

MY EXPERIENCE WITH PEER REVIEW

After completing an interventional cardiology fellowship in Phoenix in 2018, I went on to do a six-month sub-specialty fellowship in peripheral and endovascular disease, working with one of the pioneers of interventional cardiology. I then accepted a job in a suburb of Phoenix, joining a three-physician private practice group. As part of the new job, I was required to acquire privileges at four of the hospitals that the group covered in the surrounding Phoenix area.

Since I was new out of fellowship, I figured this privileging process would be straightforward, which was true for three of the four hospitals. One hospital was a heart hospital that was primarily covered by a 30-cardiologist private practice group and three other small (1–3 doctors) groups, including the group I joined.

The 30-cardiology physician group dominated the marketplace in the area. I encountered difficulties obtaining hospital privileges at this heart hospital from the beginning of the privileging process.

After submitting the initial credentialing application, the credentialing committee, which was comprised of many cardiologists from the large private practice heart group, met and decided that because I had a gap in my medical training (I took an academic leave of absence in medical school and worked in a translational science lab), they wanted to see my medical school dean's letter. I quickly submitted a copy of the dean's letter, but this was not sufficient, as they needed an official copy from my medical school.

At the following month's medical executive committee (MEC) meeting, the credentialing committee decided that they wanted to interview me in person. The next month, I was told the committee "tabled" my application to the following month's meeting since they did not have enough time to discuss my request for privileges.

At their next MEC meeting, they requested that I get a hair and urine drug screen. I am not sure why they did not request that earlier if they knew that a hair and urine drug screen is something that they required for hospital privileging. I was getting increasingly frustrated with the entire privileging process, as were my partners who had to cover patients at that heart hospital on days I was on-call.

After getting the drug screen, I was finally approved at their next meeting, but with several conditions:

- I was not granted peripheral vascular privileges even though I had done additional training in peripheral and endovascular interventions because my training was not part of an ACGME accredited fellowship. My attempts to explain to the credentialing committee that there are no ACGME accredited fellowships for peripheral artery, or structural interventions, or imaging fell on deaf ears. Not having basic privileges for peripheral interventions puts an interventional cardiologist at a disadvantage, especially for complex procedures where one may need to treat a bleeding groin complication, for example.

- I was not granted privileges for coronary atherectomy and mechanical circulatory support device placement — skills that are required in order to graduate from any interventional fellowship — and was told I could reapply months later when the committee could review my coronary interventional cases. They might reconsider my application for privileges then.

With these restrictions, I started covering that heart hospital. There were some inconveniences, as for any procedure requiring atherectomy, I had to stop the procedure after taking the diagnostic images, take them off the table, and reschedule them at one of the other hospitals our group covered.

One morning, I did a cardiac catheterization on an outpatient with angina and inferior wall ischemia on stress testing. A right radial approach was attempted, but was unsuccessful, as the patient had aberrant arterial anatomy. Ultrasound-guided right common femoral artery access was then obtained.

After the percutaneous coronary intervention was complete, the scrub tech attempted to close the arteriotomy site with a closure device. Most cardiology physicians will let a staff member close the groin site, as most are proficient in it, and it demonstrates their confidence in the staff.

Unfortunately, the technician was unsuccessful. I scrubbed back in and deployed the closure device. At this point, the patient was noted to be significantly hypotensive, blood pressure as low as 69/44mmHg, and despite receiving 300mcg IV of phenylephrine to increase the blood pressure, his BP only went up to 90s mm Hg systolic.

I was concerned that the patient had a retroperitoneal bleed due to excessive manipulation of the groin when that scrub tech attempted to insert the closure device. I needed to get access into the contralateral artery and perform an aortogram to evaluate for a life-threatening bleed. Time was critical, and I asked someone else to scrub in and help, as the initial scrub tech was shaking and having some difficulty with the wires.

Someone else stepped in, and the first tech scrubbed out. While all this was going on, I was worried about what I was going to do if there was a retroperitoneal bleed because although they can be treated, I did not have privileges to do peripheral cases.

Thankfully, the patient did not have a bleed, the blood pressure improved, and the episode was likely due to a vasovagal reaction. I thought that the scrub tech technician had left the lab, and I said, "If she didn't feel comfortable closing the groin, she should have said so initially." The tech was still in the room and, clearly upset, told me she has a lot of experience.

Afterward, several of the cath lab staff were angry with me for asking the cath lab tech to scrub out of the case, as "she has 20 years of experience." I apologized to the entire cath lab staff and personally apologized to the tech I asked to scrub out. She accepted my apology, but later I found out the lab was going to "write me up."

I truly did not intend to be disrespectful or offend anyone. I was disheartened that I was going to be written up, as I felt the staff knew me, would understand that it was a stressful situation for me, and would be more understanding and forgiving.

A month after this incident, I was asked to meet with the president of the medical staff as well as the chief medical officer. I was apologetic and thought the meeting went well, but a few days later found out that it would be escalated to the MEC.

The MEC was comprised of members from the large cardiology practice. The partners in my group advised me to retain an attorney.

My attorney had represented a lot of clients over the years who had issues with the MEC. These clients, similar to me, were attempting to practice on the cardiology turf of the large heart hospital group. The attorney advised that we be proactive and recommended that I take a three-day "Elevating Civility and Communication" course as well as an eight-hour counseling session with a psychologist who works specifically with physicians. I followed both of these recommendations.

The MEC required that I sign a stipulation agreement for "concerns relating to physician's inappropriate conduct," essentially stating that any further issue would have significant consequences. Just two weeks later, I received another letter from the chief of staff regarding a patient care concern about a patient whom I did not see, and indicated that it was an issue that would be escalated to the MEC.

With regard to the issue, one of my partners did a pacemaker generator exchange on an 85-year-old patient on a Thursday afternoon when I was on vacation. He did not check this patient out to me on Thursday as I was on vacation, and he placed orders for the patient to be discharged Friday morning.

On Friday morning, the nurse informed me that the patient's son refused to take the patient home because he wanted his father to be evaluated by physical therapy. This was the first I had learned about this patient, and the request was reasonable, so the nurse took a telephone order for physical therapy, and I did not think anything more of it.

That evening at 8:30 pm, I received a page that physical therapy was unable to evaluate the patient and that his home medications needed to be ordered, which I did. The patient went home Saturday morning.

I was asked to provide a written response explaining why the patient was not seen by me, "the covering physician." I explained the circumstances to the MEC and indicated that typically for patients that was "outpatient" status and as discharge orders were in place, a daily progress note was not required.

The MEC disagreed with me and I was required to sign an addendum to the prior stipulation agreement stating: "Physician acknowledges that Physician's failure to comply with the terms of this agreement will be deemed cause for immediate termination of Physician's medical staff membership and privileges."

As someone who was fresh out of fellowship and excited about cardiology, I was upset by the fact that everything I had worked so hard for could be so easily taken away from me. My attorney advised that I request a leave of absence from that hospital, and that as soon as all investigations were over, I resign, which is what I did. I met another interventional cardiologist who also had issues with that heart hospital. He decided to sue, but despite spending $500,000 and several years of litigation, he ultimately lost.

Unfortunately, I've learned that regardless of the circumstances, the MEC has the final say. There is no one else to go to because all MEC matters are confidential. Every letter I got was marked with "Privileged and Confidential Peer Review Information A.R.S. 36.445 et seq. and 36.2401 et. seq."

Sadly, a process meant to protect patients can be used to thwart competition and possibly destroy a physician's practice life. I felt the sword placed in my heart by the MEC, and I was left scared, depressed, and pessimistic about whether there was a true due process in peer review.

PRACTICING IN A COMPLEX WORLD

The following physician's story is meant to help the reader understand the complexity of practicing medicine in the world of corporate medicine.

"Trust nobody, assume nothing" was the inspiring advice I received from my boss after asking his advice on how to handle an error made by the hospital administration. The hospital had settled a lawsuit with a patient for a very small amount; however, based on internal policies, any settlement of more than $2,500 required a review to determine if the physician should be reported to the National Practitioner Data Bank.

Seemed like a reasonable process that would apply fairly to all, but there was only one problem: I was not the surgeon of record for this patient. How did they get my name? How did the hospital administration and legal team allow this to happen? Surely this would be very easy to clear up: I would show them the operative dictation and explain that although I was trained to perform a thyroidectomy, I hadn't done the procedure in several years.

I started with my chief of surgery (my boss), then risk management, then hospital counsel, and my personal attorney. I did not anticipate that what I believed was a clerical error was really a decision on the part of my boss to assign a complication to me because one of his golden boys was having a run of complications. I could never have imagined that a system could exist that would allow an error to pass through multiple layers of review all the way to a financial settlement. I could never imagine that once the error was identified that the error would remain because it would expose the corruption that was in the system. I could never imagine that when I wrote my letter defending myself, the most basic human right, the chief of staff would chastise me for being selfish and not thinking of the institution first.

It wasn't until a few years later that I realized the question that I never asked and didn't have the answer to: Why would my boss protect Dr. X and not me? What is he bringing to the table that I am not? Who does he know? Who is he friends with? Who is protecting him?

The practice of medicine rewards us all with more than we can measure on earth. However, medicine is also a high-pressure environment, filled with competition and large salaries. All of the ingredients for greed and poor discretion run wild.

"WE ALL HAVE THE SAME CONTRACT."

I was a new surgeon looking for jobs when I came across a very busy hospital system in the middle of nowhere. The managing partner and senior partner of the group took me to dinner and began the sales pitch of why I should join them. Of all the things they told me that night, the one topic that made the greatest impression on me was that we are all equal and we all have the same contract. I couldn't believe that was true: How could two gentlemen at least 20 years into their respective practices take as much call and make the same salary as a new surgeon starting out. Certainly, I was naïve, but I believed I was very smart and I had a lawyer.

This was my first lesson in the difference between telling the truth and telling the whole truth. One of the perks of working all the nights and weekends as the junior partner was seeing what came across the fax machine at night. We all had the same identical contract, but the senior guys had a separate compensation plan for productivity as well as a progressive call compensation plan for covering vacations, sick leave, and parental leave. My favorite was the back-up pay that the senior guys were receiving for being such gracious mentors.

I talked things over with my lawyer and he told me that I didn't have much that I could do except move on. I took a few months to think about what to do, and I was actually leaning toward staying until they went one step too far.

One of our CV surgeons was leaving and was selling his spectacular condo that I quickly made a deal to purchase. It was a cash purchase that I convinced my parents to loan me the money to close quickly. It was springtime, sunny outside and things looked a little brighter for me until I made the mistake of sharing the news of my good fortune with my senior partner.

By the end of the week, the condo deal fell through and the condo was sold to someone else. The CV surgeon stopped taking my calls and the real estate agent was not responding either until I threatened to file a complaint against them. The real estate agent called me back and told me that I should let it go because my senior partner is the one who bought the apartment. He told the real estate agent that I didn't deserve to buy that unique opportunity, and that I needed to wait my turn.

I made the decision to leave, and when I provided my notice through the appropriate channels, I discovered the power of the Focused Professional Practice Evaluation (FPPE) and Ongoing Professional Practice Evaluation (OPPE) processes and peer review. Needless to say, I was able to leave without a mark on my record, but I did so only after covering the entire summer and the winter holidays. They kept my bonus, denied me parental leave that was part of benefits package, and refused to pay any of my CME expenses. It was the best $150,000 that I ever spent on my education. Lesson learned.

"YOU ARE MY RIGHT HAND. YOU ARE OUR NEXT STAR!"

I joined a growing program with a senior partner who was going to help me become a fast surgeon so that I could double my caseload. Even better: I was going to work one week less per month and earn a base salary of $75,000 more per year. There was even a new hospital under construction closer to my home, and I was the Prince in waiting. I was on my second contract and thought I was negotiating more for my value. How could I lose?

Turns out I was a double agent and didn't know it. My partner was pushing for a partner so that he could have every Thursday night through Sunday off. The hospital administration hired me as part of the plan to reduce the compensation plan for my partner by putting me at odds with him. Now it didn't take me long to figure out the plan, and I even figured out a simple solution: vacation time. I used my vacation time as a weapon to fight back against both. He got what he wanted and had the weekends off, I created an alternative that I could live with and for a little while life was better. The administration was not pleased that they left a loophole for me to escape the turmoil.

They quietly moved into plan B: Use their other surgeons to attack my partner and me together. Lucky for me, I didn't have enough time in the system for the committees to work their dark magic, but for my partner, they had boxes of paperwork to pull from.

Again, I was left with only the power of my feet to make a move out of a bad situation. I found another job and literally moved out of my office at night. The distance and strain on my family life was worse than before and even though I left with a clean record and gave the appropriate notice, I was marked a "do not hire."

In the end, I don't have any regrets of navigating myself out of a bad situation, but the people who masterminded a plan filled with ill intentions still found a way to put a mark on my record.

"THIS IS A GREAT PLACE TO RAISE KIDS, MY WIFE AND I MOVED HERE 3 YEARS AGO, AND WE ARE NEVER LEAVING."

I took a new job as a director and I was required to work only one week a month for the same amount I was making at my previous job. Even better, the hospital was going through a change over from a private model to an employed model. I was going to get my chance to perform all of the cases that I wanted, I would get my choice of call, I would have a chance to run things on my terms.

There was only one problem: I was the only employed physician and full time meant all the time. I was hired to do the work that eight physicians were doing. Ok, no problem: I will go to the CEO and tell him the obvious and he will make it right. A few rounds of negotiating and we shared a gentleman's handshake over dinner.

The next week the CEO accepted a job in Florida and I embarked on three years and 12 different CEOs. There wasn't a lot of betrayal in this experience, but the lesson I learned was that I was distracted by the toxicity of my previous experience and that I didn't ask the questions that I needed to ask.

"TIME TO GRAB THE BRASS RING!"

Now, a seasoned surgeon into my fourth contract and I was asked by a friend to help him out with coverage at a hospital just 45 minutes from my house. The pitch: We all make the same amount, we are all equals, and we all have a say in the schedule. I decided to wait a little and let things play out. No need to rush myself; I was moving up the ladder and I had the scars to prove it.

I needed something more than just money and with time it came: I was named director of a group of 30 surgeons, nurse practitioners, and physician assistants. To say that I wasn't full of myself would be a lie: I felt that I belonged in my new role. I was an experienced surgeon with no lawsuits, every employer had a hardworking employee that had exceeded all of the productivity targets that were set, performance bonuses were always earned (not paid), and I had embarked on graduate training in healthcare administration.

What was missing is that I had lost perspective of what I had given up. I became the employee that I never wanted to become: I was now a "yes" man, working day and night, vulnerable to everyone above and below me. My physical health suffered, my mental health suffered, my personal life suffered, but I was delivering on every task that was put in front of me. I immersed myself in this position convinced that I would make this opportunity the one that counts.

While working day and night for three years with only 12 days off in total, I nearly died in a horrible car accident that left me permanently injured. When I called my boss after the accident to tell him that I was in the hospital, he was on a golf course with the other administrators and the only question he had for me was whether I was going to be able to take call that night.

Two weeks later, I was asked to see him in a meeting with the CEO. Instead of asking me if I was ok, they chastised me for not supporting another struggling service line. Challenge accepted! They buried me under so much work that I wasn't watching what was going on around me. My friend, my partner, was the golden boy they always wanted. He was the master puppeteer and he brought me in to get the job done that he couldn't do. All the while, he was setting up to take over after I built the program that they wanted.

Sure enough, I attained American College of Surgeons Verification, I recruited a full team of employed surgeons, I modernized the service, I did the fund raising to buy new equipment, the outreach to grow the service 288% year over year. On Friday, I was called into the office and given the "compassion" award, and the following Thursday, I was told the organization was going in a different direction.

When I shared my story with friends and family, all of them told me it was my partner who had been working in the shadows while I was submerged in the sea of toxic waste. I refused to believe it. He was my friend, we made a lot of money together, we did a lot of good work together, and there was no benefit to taking me out. Boy was I wrong.

He was able to negotiate a larger contract, with less work and full autonomy to run the team. The therapy for this was six months of working out, finding a new job, and even having the time and opportunity to write this paragraph. I was procrastinating and avoiding putting my thoughts down on paper until it happened again.

January 30, 2023: I am now working with a CEO to build a surgical program close to my hometown. It's time to give back, serve the people, but I had to make sure that I was compensated fairly without interference. It was a quick negotiation that I was trying to be fair and upfront with my needs absent greed. I just wanted distance from my past, and I wanted to be someplace where my work would mean something.

"WE ARE PART OF A BIG CONGLOMERATE OF HOSPITALS, ALL OF OUR SURGEONS GET THE SAME CONTRACT, AND WE CAN'T MAKE TOO MANY CHANGES. YOU HAVE MY WORD ON THIS."

I knew that was all nonsense, but the contract came and it was simple and short. Legal turnaround was easy and I signed on. After sacrificing my long overdue vacation with my family performing the obligatory new guy holiday coverage, I was speaking with my new colleagues about some surgeons we were recruiting when I learned that the contract negotiations were moving at lightning speed.

The CEO had given the new surgeons the contract terms that I had proposed a few months prior. I couldn't believe it, so I did what any self-respecting individual would do. I celebrated the win and I spread the word that we had signed two surgeons and that they were excited to join. It didn't take long for the CEO to ask to meet with me. When I did, he looked me straight in the eye and congratulated me on the work and told me he was appreciative of me not making a big deal out of things.

I was stunned. Here was a guy admitting to me that he lied and expecting me to let things go as "business as usual." I almost let it go until he told me that he consulted with my previous partner on how to approach me about this issue and my partner advised him that I would not raise any issue, just as I hadn't with my partner.

In that moment, I knew that I never had a chance and it was time to take control of my destiny. What does that mean? I still have no idea, but the mindset of having the curtains pulled back, the band-aids ripped off, and knowing that my efforts will never be rewarded has liberated me from my own constraints and hopefully with time I will find a clear path forward.

SECTION 3

Fiduciary, Trustee, Professional

This section will outline the fiduciary duty of every physician practicing medicine (Chapters 10–12).

CHAPTER 10

The Physician Fiduciary: Understanding Trusteeship

Physicians, acting as fiduciaries and trustees to patients, have a physician–patient relationship. That physician–patient relationship will lead to high-quality medical care, excellent health outcomes, and contained medical costs. Responsible physicians must understand the importance of being a fiduciary and trustee to their patients in a complex healthcare arena that has changed from palpable public responsibilities to a profit-maximization business model.

PHYSICIAN TRUSTEE AND FIDUCIARY

As physicians, we operate in a complex, ever-changing medical landscape. The goal of maximizing profits percolated into the healthcare sector that was once based on the "common good" of our patients and society. What is the common good? It consists of our communal values, about what we owe one another as citizens, bound together in the same society seeking the rules and principles we seek to achieve together. A concern for the moral good is an ethical attitude that recognizes that we are all in it together. If there is no common good, there is no society.

A century ago, hospitals and health insurers had palpable public responsibilities. The original purpose of health insurance plans, devised at Baylor University in the 1920s, was not to maximize profits. The original intent of the health insurance plan was to share the risk of illness across all demographics and to cover as many people as possible (maximize the common good).

The nonprofit Blue Cross and Blue Shield accepted everyone who wanted to be a member. Unique to this plan was the idea that every member paid the same rate, irrespective of age or health. In the 1960s, Blue Cross was providing hospital coverage to more than 50 million Americans.

In the 1970s, "entrepreneurs" seized an opportunity to make vast sums of money by exploiting the common good. This change in the health insurance landscape adulterated the charitable mission of Blue Cross and Blue Shield. These entrepreneurs founded for-profit insurance companies like Aetna and Cigna that accepted only younger and healthier patients. This profit-driven mission allowed them to lower their premiums below the Blues while running to their depository with hefty profits.

The Blues were unable to compete, so in 1994, they surrendered and became for-profit. This ended the era of nonprofit health insurance. This tragic transition led to a new paradigm where the American health insurance system zealously insured the healthful and avoided the sick population. When the only motive is to make as much money as possible in the shortest time frame, the common good is easily displaced.

As physicians, we have been thrust into this dismal situation of trying to identify how we reinstate the common good back into the healthcare of America. A daunting challenge, but one that physicians must accept individually and as a group. The present-day healthcare pact has put physicians in a triangle of administration, healthcare providers, and patients.

We must resist the urge to become tribal. Tribalism is the behavior and attitudes that stem from strong loyalty to one's own tribe or social group. As physicians, we must understand the cultural, political, and financial identities of the stakeholder sitting at the healthcare policy-making table. We must act as leaders through trusteeship.

What is a trustee? Trustee is a legal term that, in its broadest sense, is a synonym for anyone in a position of trust or responsibility for the benefit of another. Physicians are the trustees of patients. Physician leaders must be the stewards of the once unwritten rules we took for granted: the common good.

Fifty years ago, healthcare leaders understood that corporations were not just for shareholders, but also for employees, communities, customers, and the public. Health insurers existed to provide coverage to everyone who needed it, not by cherry-picking the young and healthy.

Over time and through tumultuous change in the healthcare arena, leaders seem to have forgotten that their legitimacy depends on advancing the common good and that this type of leadership is a public trust. Trusteeship should be inoculated into the understanding of successful physician leadership. Physician leadership must teach every physician the importance of being a fiduciary/trustee in the doctor–patient relationship.

Physicians have a duty to meet in an open-minded manner with administrators and patients to discuss how to achieve solutions that restore the common good in healthcare. The lack of a common good strategy will harm everyone over time. The job of the physician leader is to help educate all stakeholders.

This is not simply about ethics. Ethics involves fulfilling legal responsibilities and avoiding obvious conflicts of interest. Physician leadership should not play to win the lottery, but to serve the common good of our nation. If physicians understand this trusteeship, they are in a unique position to restore the common good in healthcare. Leadership as trusteeship extends beyond ethics. It requires a different way of thinking about the central obligation of leaders. Its essence is restoring trust in the healthcare system.

CHAPTER 11

Physician Professionalism

Professionalism is the basis of medicine's social agreement with society. This contractual relationship demands placing the interests of patients above those of physicians, setting and maintaining extraordinary standards of competence and integrity, and delivering knowledgeable and professional advice to society on matters of health and well-being.

The medical profession is being challenged by an eruption of technology, fluctuating market forces, and problems in ever-changing healthcare delivery. The exponential transformations across an array of technology and market changes make it a real task for physicians to meet their obligations to patients. Indeed, the medical profession must contend with political, legal, and market forces that challenge physicians to meet their fiduciary responsibility to their patients.

The fundamental principles inherent to physician professionalism include patient welfare, patient autonomy, and elimination of discrimination in healthcare, whether based on race, gender, socioeconomic status, ethnicity, or religion. Market forces, societal pressures, and administrative exigencies must not compromise the principles inherent in a true physician–patient relationship.

Physicians must be sincere and trustworthy with patients and empower them to make informed decisions about their treatment options. Patient decisions about their medical care must be paramount, as long as the care is ethical and the patient's decision does not lead to demands for incongruous care given the clinical presentation.

Discussed here are the necessary physician professional responsibilities, the medical and legal fiduciary obligations of physicians, and how employed physicians caught in a web of ascendant market focus may be wedged in a conundrum of how to maintain patient primacy and their own professional responsibilities.

PROFESSIONAL RESPONSIBILITIES

Physician professional responsibilities should encompass a commitment to professional competence, integrity with patients, patient confidentiality, preservation of appropriate personal and financial relations, access to medical care, highest quality medical healthcare, equitable distribution of finite resources, and maintaining trust by never succumbing to conflict of interests for personal or financial gain.

Physicians must be devoted to lifelong learning and maintaining the knowledge and skills to provide standard-of-care medicine. Education is crucial in the world of ever-advancing medical knowledge, and all physicians should pursue continuing medical education to maintain the highest level of competence in their area of practice.

Medical informed consent is essential to a true patient-physician relationship. Patients need to participate in the informed consent process to understand the risk-benefit relationship for the proposed treatment strategy; this understanding is essential because patients are often psychologically regressed when confronted severe illness, realizing that they are confronting a life-preserving procedure.

Physicians need to participate in the informed consent process to provide patients with the best treatment available by sharing decision-making and limiting any potential for liability. Medical ethics, common law, and, in many states, codified statutory law mandate the informed consent process. Physicians should be knowledgeable in the areas of medical ethics, common law, and statutory law.

Whenever patients are injured as a result of medical care, the physician should immediately inform the patient and family because failure to inform them compromises patient and societal trust, and confidence in the medical system. Reporting and analyzing medical errors provides a basis and foundation for developing prevention and improvement strategies and apt compensation to injured parties.

Physicians are responsible for the sanctity of the patient's medical information. Patient confidentiality is critical in today's world of widespread use of electronic information systems for compiling and storing patient information and data, and the ever-increasing use of genomic information that may impact a patient's ability to obtain insurance and career opportunities.

The slippery slope to watch out for is in the exchange of information with persons acting on the patient's behalf when obtaining informed consent when the patient is not competent/capable of consenting. All conversations must be measured and well thought through. The commitment to confidentiality may occasionally be trumped by overarching considerations of public interest.

The physician–patient relationship is inherently vulnerable because illness allows patients to emotionally decompensate and become dependent upon an authority figure. Given the intrinsic vulnerability and dependency that may occur, physicians must be cognizant of the importance of never exploiting a patient sexually or for personal financial gain.

The improvement of the quality of patient care is an essential core value for every physician. Physicians must be dedicated to continuous improvement in the quality of medical healthcare. This commitment must entail maintaining personal clinical competence and requires collaboration with all colleagues to increase clinical knowledge, reduce medical errors, increase patient safety, minimize overuse/misuse of healthcare resources, and optimize patient outcomes.

Physicians have an inherent duty to participate in the development of quality of care measures and the application of quality measures to assess individuals, institutions, and systems responsible for healthcare delivery. Physicians, individually and through professional organizations, must take responsibility for assisting and maintaining mechanisms to encourage continuous improvement in knowledge and quality of care, including attempts to diminish barriers to excellent and equitable medical care.

The objective of medical care must be the availability of uniform, excellent standards of care across all demographics and socioeconomic classes.

Physicians must diligently access the just distribution of finite medical resources by providing healthcare that is based on judicious and cost-effective management of limited clinical resources and huge financial healthcare dollar deficits. The physician's professional responsibility for equitable allocation of resources requires conscientious avoidance of tests and procedures that are unnecessary and financially driven. The provision of unwarranted medical services exposes patients to risk and expense and limits the available resources for others in true need. Across profit and non-profit organizations, physicians and organizations have sundry opportunities to compromise their professional responsibilities by pursuing personal advantage.

Physicians have a duty to disclose conflicts of interest that arise in their professional work. Moreover, there is a moral and ethical duty to disclose observed, unethical behavior of physicians and medical organizations, whether acting in isolation or in concert. As part of their professional responsibility, physicians must participate in self-regulation, including remediation and punishment of physicians, administrators, and organizations that fail to meet professional standards.

FIDUCIARY RESPONSIBILITY OF PHYSICIANS

The word "fiduciary" derives from the Latin word for "trust." The covenant of trust between the patient and the physician is vital to the diagnostic and therapeutic process. It is the foundation of the physician-patient relationship. To facilitate physicians making accurate diagnoses and providing optimal therapeutic recommendations, patients must trust they can communicate all relevant information about an illness or injury without the physician divulging confidential information. The fiduciary relationship is based on accepted codes of professional ethics.

Historically, the physician–patient relationship was created upon the principle of benevolence, played out through the doctrine of medical authoritarianism. Medical paternalism eventually succumbed to notions of patient autonomy when it was determined that patients had the right to make their own decisions. This has evolved to the concept of shared responsibility where the physician and the patient jointly exercise decision-making authority.

Medical paternalism has been defined as an action taken by one person in the best interest of another without their consent. The rationale was that the physician alone possessed the knowledge and experience needed to make a medical decision; it was therapeutically counterproductive for a patient to understand their compromised state of health and the risks they faced because it would jeopardize, limit and retard recovery. Paternalism pervaded the physician–patient relationship until the middle of the 20th century.

In 1914, in *Schloendorff v. Society of New York Hospital*, Justice Benjamin Cardozo wrote, "Every human being of adult years and sound mind has a right to determine what shall be done with his own body; and a surgeon who performs an operation without his patient's consent commits an assault." His landmark decision marked a radical shift toward recognizing patients' rights in the physician-patient relationship. The increased recognition of civil rights in the 1960s permeated and enhanced a range of individual rights, including those of medical patients. The courts ultimately endorsed the position that a physician would be liable if there was failure to obtain informed consent before medical or surgical treatment.

In the seminal case of *Canterbury v. Spence*, the court ruled that a physician has a duty to disclose to a patient the material risk associated with a proposed therapy that a reasonable patient would need to hear to make an informed decision. The informed consent requirement marked the zenith of the shift in the nature of the physician-patient relationship from paternalistic to autonomous patient.

Today the pendulum has swung to a position of shared decision-making. Proper healthcare decision-making and management involves a detailed communication and exchange between patients and physicians where the patient shares their symptoms, concerns, goals, personal and family history, and lifestyle desires; the physicians share the risks, side effects, alternative approaches to care, and potential outcomes. This is a two-way exchange that represents a true physician-patient partnership.

Informed consent is a physician's obligation to the patient ethically, morally, and legally. The term "informed consent" was coined and explained in *Salgo v. Leland Stanford Jr. University Board of Trustees*, where a California Court of Appeals declared that "a physician violates his duty to his patient and subjects himself to liability if he withholds any facts which are necessary to form the basis of an intelligent consent by the patient to the proposed treatment." Subsequent to this ruling, informed consent became an ethical and legal duty imposed upon physicians throughout the United States.

Physicians now consider informed consent a fundamental component of healthcare that is universally accepted. Physicians now have an ethical and legal responsibility to inform patients of the potential material risks and benefits of any proposed treatment before obtaining a patient's consent to perform a medical procedure, with the patient given the right to make the ultimate decision of the course of treatment. The duty of physicians to the patient is ethically, morally, and legally sacrosanct. This duty is a critical piece of the professional responsibilities of physicians.

In a world exploding with medical information through television advertising and the internet, physicians must know how to respond to informed patients. Physicians often encounter requests for medical care that is not medically necessary by patients who have misinterpreted the information on the internet or advertising. Physicians should not lose sight of their prime fiduciary responsibility to promote and protect the best interests of the patient, even at the risk of losing revenue. The law empowers physicians to say no to services that are not medically indicated, an empowerment that serves society well.

THE THREAT TO PHYSICIAN PROFESSIONALISM

Patients have experienced a transition from paternalism to autonomous decision-making. Physicians have experienced a transition from autonomy to conflict as to who is their fiduciary. Physicians progressively practice as employees of large corporate medical organizations. Ascendant market fundamentalism has pressured physicians to practice as a fiduciary to the organization. Employed physicians report to business-trained managers and may be subject to contractual obligations that threaten quality of care, patient safety, and the professional and fiduciary responsibilities they owe patients.

Numerous provisions in physicians' contracts interfere with physician professional responsibilities and fiduciary duties. In the new era of employed physicians, problematic contractual clauses impeding physicians' professional duties and fiduciary responsibilities include the following.

- *Confidentiality clauses:* Confidentiality clauses in physician contracts often attempt to hide quality and safety issues, medical errors, unethical conduct, and malfeasance. These confidentiality clauses are in direct opposition to physicians' professional responsibility to improve the quality of patient care. Physicians must be dedicated to continuous improvement in the quality of medical care. This commitment must entail reducing all medical errors, increasing patient safety, minimizing overuse and misuse of healthcare resources, and optimizing patient outcomes. Physicians have an inherent duty to participate in the development of quality of care measures and the application of quality measures to assess individuals, institutions, and systems responsible for healthcare delivery. The objective of medical care must be the availability of uniform and excellent standard of care across all demographics and socioeconomic classes. The confidentiality clause can prevent physicians from meeting the professional, ethical, and moral responsibilities necessary to maintain the fiduciary responsibilities inherent in a physician-patient relationship.

- *Incentive clauses*: Most physician contracts include productivity incentives. Physicians have been terminated for low productivity or for not meeting these incentives. These clauses provide inducements for activities that primarily increase employer income and tend to inspire overtreatment, in direct opposition to physicians' professional responsibility to diligently access the just distribution of finite medical resources. Physicians must provide healthcare that is based on judicious and cost-effective management of limited clinical resources and huge financial healthcare dollar deficits, requiring conscientious avoidance of tests and procedures that are unnecessary and financially driven. The provision of unwarranted medical services exposes patients to risk and expense and limits the available resources for others in true need.

- *Referral restrictions*: Referral restrictions are referred to as "leakage control." Many physician contracts prohibit referring outside the system, which prohibits appropriate referrals for particular patients, thus decreasing quality of care. Many physician offices have physician navigators who direct the care of patients to specialists in the health system and take the control of referral away from the primary physician. Contractual clauses interfering with referral to skilled, elite physicians directly oppose the professional responsibility of physicians to assist and maintain mechanisms to encourage continuous improvement in quality of care. Physicians must collectively attempt to diminish barriers to excellent, equitable medical care.

- *"Gag" clauses and termination without cause:* Clauses that prohibit physicians from revealing quality and safety problems, medical errors, and unethical conduct, and bar physicians from revealing problems with electronic medical records that result in healthcare quality and safety issues (often emanating from confidentiality clauses in the contracts between hospital employers and electronic record vendors) directly interfere with a physician's professional responsibilities. Clauses allowing termination without cause put physicians at extreme risk for standing up for professional responsibilities and to maintaining their fiduciary responsibility to the patient when it conflicts with the employer. The gag clauses and termination without cause clauses are in direct opposition to physicians' commitment to reduce medical errors, increase patient safety, minimize overuse and misuse of healthcare resources, optimize patient outcomes, and stand up to the organization when behaviors surface that interfere with physician professionalism and fiduciary responsibility.

THE CONUNDRUM PHYSICIANS FACE

Physicians are juxtaposed between professional responsibilities and contractual obligations that limit their ability to meet professional responsibilities, and their fiduciary responsibility to their patients. This juxtaposition results from manifestations of corporate medicine, letting the demands of the marketplace undermine the goals of professional and fiduciary responsibility of physicians.

The ascendant market fundamentalism has pressured physicians to become entrepreneurial businesspersons rather than professionals. This shift in the physician's fiduciary responsibility to the employer threatens the quality of care, patient safety, and physician professional values.

It is a daunting time for physicians, patients, and society. Given that the managers of large health corporations may not be willing to meaningfully negotiate the most egregious provisions in the contractual relationship with individual physicians leaves physicians feeling impotent, as these corporate demands are common across employers. The intransigence of these organizations reflects their sheer market dominance.

What can physicians do to combat this provoked loss of professional values and fiduciary responsibility? They must demand a return to professional values and fiduciary responsibility to the patient. Perhaps this may require physicians to organize to collectively bargain with uncompromising and unyielding employers.

CHAPTER 12

Medical Ethics: Medical Legal Issues Surrounding Advance Directives and the Power of Attorney

This chapter will share a wide swath of private practice patterns observed in private practice cardiology. Many aspects of cardiology practice will be reviewed, including clinical cardiology practice, cardiac catheterization, echocardiography, stress testing, ECG interpretation, Holter monitoring, outreach cardiology clinics, heart failure clinic, cardiology leadership, and cardiac surgery.

There will be a discussion of the guideline-directed indications for the different testing modalities and the misappropriation of these tests in today's cost-conscious medical environment. These observations of excessive testing point out the areas in dire need of improvement through measuring what matters, honest review of limitations of the present practice patterns, and the responses to adverse outcomes.

Before addressing the practice patterns observed in private practice medicine, let's review the main principles of clinical medical ethics.

Medical ethics is not just about right and wrong. It is a rigorous academic discipline combing philosophy, history, sociology, and theology, which help the clinician, navigate the complex moral choices that are increasingly common in the modern era of medical practice.

Healthcare is faced with the "tragedy of the commons," and four values provide a framework from which clinicians can argue for balanced decision-making:

- Respect for autonomy
- Beneficence (physician acting as the patient's fiduciary)
- Non-maleficence: "Do no harm"
- Justice

Determining who is incapacitated is challenging, and the nomenclature is confusing. While the words capacity and competence are used interchangeably, capacity is different than competence from a legal perspective. Capacity is a medical term used by the treating physician, while competence is considered a legal term and is determined by the court system.

According to strict legal definitions, competence refers to global decision-making. It is wider ranging than capacity, or the ability to make decisions about medical therapy. The distinction is important, and these terms are both important in determining how to help patients who may not be able to help themselves in times of medical need. There are four key components to capacity: the ability to communicate a choice, the ability to understand the medical risks and benefits, appreciation of what they are deciding, and demonstration of rational thought and reasoning.

Capacity is the underpinning and basis for informed consent. Informed consent is essential to the doctor–patient relationship where the physician acts as the patient's fiduciary. Patients must demonstrate the capacity to make medical decisions related to their own well-being. If the patient can demonstrate their understanding of the medical condition, appreciate the consequences of the decisions they are making, display reasoning in their thought process, and effectively communicate their wishes, then in most situations, they will be considered to have demonstrated capacity.

More than a million people have died from COVID infections since the pandemic began; many of them did not have advance medical directives indicating how they wanted healthcare decisions to be made if they were unable to express their desires. As a result, families struggled to determine the best approach to end-of-life care for their loved ones.

Advance directives guide the medical team to provide medical care and alleviate the burden on families to decide what types of medical care and treatment the patient would want. The two forms of advance directives that physicians should discuss with families are the power of attorney for healthcare and the declaration to physicians (the living will).

These and other documents discussed in this chapter are available on the Internet and at some retail stores; however, if they are to be used for legal purposes, they must be notarized and properly filed.

THE POWER OF ATTORNEY FOR HEALTHCARE

The Power of Attorney (POA) for Healthcare is an important legal concept in managing the medical care of patients who no longer have the capacity to make their own healthcare decisions. There are four types of POAs: limited POA restricted to specified issues, general POA, springing POA that becomes active when the patient becomes incapacitated, and co-POA for the successor who takes over when the general POA is absent. A POA who does not act in good faith as a fiduciary for the patient may be subject to liability.

If patients lose the ability to make their own healthcare decisions (loss of capacity), the Power of Attorney for Healthcare designates an agent who, in collaboration with the personal physician, can make healthcare decisions for a patient. Additionally, the patient may complete a Power of Health Care addendum, which outlines treatment preferences and desires that will guide the designated healthcare agent's decision-making.

The healthcare agent can advise the patient's personal physician, physicians providing medical care, and the hospital staff on what medical treatment the patient wants in all anticipated healthcare end-of-life situations.

If the Power of Attorney for Healthcare has been completed correctly, this advance directive can, in most cases, prevent a court-supervised guardianship or a protective placement proceeding. For this reason, it is often preferable to consult an attorney who can write, or review, the document as it applies to the individual situation. The Power of Attorney for Healthcare may prevent heated debates between family and healthcare providers and costly guardianship proceedings in court. It is a more robust document than the Declaration to Physicians because it can include an addendum specifying treatment preferences.

THE DECLARATION TO PHYSICIANS

The Declaration to Physicians describes the life-sustaining medical care to be given to a patient with a terminal condition or who is in a persistent vegetative state. The declaration guides the physicians and healthcare team in deciding whether to withhold or withdraw life-sustaining treatment, such as a feeding tube, if the patient cannot be "cured" and death is imminent. However, the Declaration to Physicians does not give physicians or other healthcare providers authority to make healthcare decisions on the patient's behalf.

A court-supervised guardianship and protective placement proceeding are required if the patient is moved to a nursing facility. Such action would be covered under a Power of Attorney for Healthcare directive. The court establishes guardianship because it has determined the ward is not competent. Guardianship requires accounting and reporting to the court and differs from the POA in that a guardianship cannot be cancelled.

When there is no one to assume the healthcare agent role or the agent becomes incapacitated or dies, the Declaration to Physicians is the next best option. If a patient has both types of advance directives, they should be consistent; if there is any conflict, the Power of Attorney for Healthcare will prevail.

Physicians have a fiduciary duty to educate patients regarding all options available for end-of-life medical care as patients, physicians, and families explore together the patients' wishes for end-of-life treatment.

Concerning life-saving measures, physicians should instruct patients that cardiopulmonary resuscitation (CPR) is an emergency medical procedure designed to restart the heartbeat and breathing. If CPR does not revive the patient, the emergency team may initiate advanced cardiac life support (ACLS), which may include shocking the heart, inserting a breathing tube into the trachea, and administering intravenous medications in an attempt to support life.

The patient's medical condition plays a critical role in determining the success of CPR and ACLS. If the patient's medical condition warrants a discussion of such procedures, the physician should detail the best approaches.

A do not resuscitate (DNR) order applies to patients who suffer from a terminal medical condition or a medical condition such as severe heart, lung, kidney, or brain disease that makes it highly unlikely CPR would be successful.

To be eligible for a DNR bracelet, patients with the described medical conditions must be at least 18 years of age and not be pregnant. The patient and the physician must sign an order for a DNR status; when approved, the physician, or representative agent, places the bracelet on the patient's wrist.

Mentally competent patients can revoke a DNR order by communicating to their family, agent, or physician that they wish to revoke the DNR order and remove the bracelet. Ideally, this action to revoke the DNR order should be a written document entered into the medical record and acknowledged by the family, the agent, and the physician.

Emergency responders are prohibited from performing chest compressions, inserting airways, administering cardiac resuscitation drugs, or applying electric shock therapy on DNR patients. Emergency responders are allowed to clear airways, administer oxygen, position the patient for comfort, provide pain medications, control bleeding, splint injured bones, and provide emotional support.

WHY AN ADVANCE DIRECTIVE IS ESSENTIAL

Advance directives are often prepared under the guidance of an attorney familiar with individuals who wish to make clear their end-of-life wishes to family, friends, and healthcare professionals while mentally competent. These directives prevent conflict among family members and/or physicians about the treatment the patient should receive if incapacitated and offer an advantage to healthcare providers and family members.

Physicians should stress to patients that if they become incapacitated and do not have an advance directive, no one has the legal authority to make their medical decisions. Then decisions left to the physician, spouse, adult children, or court-appointed guardian might generate discord.

So long as they demonstrate their competency as adults, patients have the right to make their own decisions about medical care, including whether to accept or refuse recommended treatment and procedures.

These documents do not become relevant until patients are no longer competent to make rational decisions regarding their healthcare. For that to occur, two physicians or a physician and a psychologist must declare that the patient no longer has the capacity to make healthcare decisions.

ROLES AND RESPONSIBILITIES OF THE HEALTHCARE TEAM AND FAMILY

The patient can appoint a spouse, trusted relative, or close friend to be their healthcare agent; however, an employee or spouse of the employee of the healthcare facility where the patient resides is not eligible to be an agent. The healthcare agent must be at least 18 years old.

The patient's healthcare agent should meet with the medical team to ensure mutual understanding of the patient's healthcare status, treatment plan, and chances for recovery. A discussion of end-of-life measures will verify that everyone is on the same page.

A clear articulation of a patient's wishes will help the agent honor and protect the patient's wishes. This discussion should cover all potential issues such as using a ventilator, kidney dialysis, artificial nutrition, CPR, pain control, where the patient prefers to die, and whether the patient wants to donate their tissue and organs.

CONCLUSION

Physicians should play a pivotal role in educating patients on how they want to approach end-of-life situations and how advance directives will allow their wishes to be carried out. Physicians must understand their fiduciary duty to take an active role in their medical communities by educating patients about the benefits of advance medical directives to allow for a peaceful and harmonious end of life.

SECTION 4

Medical Malpractice Litigation

Litigation requires not only a great deal of time and effort, it can be emotionally draining. This section covers the elements of medical malpractice litigation—what physicians should expect and how they should react.

CHAPTER 13

Elements of Malpractice and Malpractice Litigation

Becoming involved in a lawsuit can be a significant event for anyone, including a physician. It can require a great deal of the physician's time and effort, can be emotionally draining, and can serve a psychological blow to the physician's professional psyche.

When legal claims arise, physicians must trust their lawyers to address them, just as patients must trust their physicians to treat disease. As with the physician-patient relationship, the effectiveness of the lawyer-client relationship depends on the physician's absolute candidness about the events surrounding the legal claim. These communications between lawyer and client are protected as confidential to encourage this necessary candor. And, just as patient compliance promotes effective treatment, a physician must heed the lawyer's advice and instructions to ensure an effective defense.

Physicians should understand the impact of a legal claim so that if a claim does arise, the physician can react appropriately and know what to expect. It focuses on the three phases of a legal claim: the pre-suit notice period, the life of a lawsuit, and trial. And, because legal claims invoke the issue of insurance, this guide initially attempts to familiarize physicians with the nature of a medical malpractice insurance policy.

The following are the basics from which physicians can build their knowledge about medical malpractice litigation.

THE MEDICAL MALPRACTICE INSURANCE POLICY

Duties of the carrier

Defense and indemnity: The carrier has two primary obligations under a medical malpractice policy: the duty to defend and the duty to indemnify.

The duty to defend requires the carrier to retain a lawyer to defend legal claims that are brought against the physician. This duty also requires the carrier to pay expenses relating to the defense. The duty to indemnify requires the carrier to pay an amount up to the policy limits for a settlement or judgment on any covered claim against the physician.

Assignment of counsel: An insurance carrier will generally retain counsel for a physician when a lawsuit is filed, although some will do so early on when the notice letter is received. Typically, the carrier will assign a lawyer who has been approved to work on its cases, and a carrier will often honor a physician's request for a specific attorney. The carrier pays the fees of the lawyer it ultimately retains. While the physician may obtain a personal lawyer in addition to counsel retained by the carrier, the carrier will not pay those fees.

Consent to settle. Some insurance policies have a "consent clause" that requires the insurance carrier to obtain the physician's consent in order to settle a case. By giving consent, the physician places the power of decision regarding settlement in the hands of the insurance company. Settlements, like adverse judgments, are reported to the National Practitioner Data Bank.

Duties of the insured physician

Prompt notice. To preserve coverage, the policy typically requires the insured to provide the carrier with prompt notice of any potential claims or lawsuits against them. An insured physician's failure to provide prompt notice could jeopardize the carrier's obligations both to defend and to indemnify. As such, with respect to coverage, it is in a physician's best interest to provide prompt notice.

Cooperation. A policy also typically contains a "cooperation clause," which requires insured physicians to cooperate in the defense of a legal claim.

PERIOD ONE: THE PRE-SUIT NOTICE

The pre-suit notice period is perhaps the most critical to understand because a physician usually receives notice of a claim and must react to it before having the benefit of a lawyer's guidance. Understanding the significance of this notice can enable a physician to respond protectively and avoid potentially harmful conduct.

The notice letter

The legal process typically begins when a physician is served with a notice letter. This is a letter from a plaintiff's attorney advising the physician of intent to bring suit. Though required by law, the notice letter is not a lawsuit, is not filed with the court, and simply places physicians on notice of potential claims against them.

Immediate notice to the carrier

Upon receipt of a notice letter, the physician must immediately notify the insurance carrier and forward to the carrier any relevant papers. Immediate notification can institute insurance coverage; delaying notification can jeopardize coverage.

A physician should also notify the carrier upon service or notice of anything resembling a legal claim, whether or not the physician has first received a notice letter. These items could include a citation, petition, discovery request, or deposition notice. The carrier is in a much better position than the physician to evaluate the effect of any material received.

A physician should also provide notice if contacted by a plaintiff's lawyer who is "generally considering" a claim or pursuing a claim against another healthcare provider. Physicians who try on their own to convince the plaintiff's lawyer they don't belong in a lawsuit can unwittingly cause adverse consequences and guarantee their own involvement in the lawsuit.

Not only can the delayed notification damage the physician's position with respect to coverage, but it prevents the opportunity for an experienced professional, either an attorney or an insurance adjuster, to evaluate this initial contact and take steps to protect the physician's interest. If contacted, the best strategy is to refrain from discussing the case and immediately call the carrier.

The patient's chart

The next immediate step the physician must take after receiving a notice letter is to pull the patient's chart and place it somewhere safe. It

is imperative that no changes be made in the chart. If a lawsuit does develop, even the *appearance* that an alteration has been made can have a devastating impact. The chart must remain exactly the same as it was before the physician had notice of the claim.

Discussing the claim

Upon receiving a notice letter, a physician may be tempted to discuss the claim with colleagues to obtain their opinions. However, if a lawsuit does develop, the physician would likely be required to recount those conversations — even those unfavorable to the physician's position. Physicians should discuss claims only with their insurance carrier and their lawyer.

PERIOD TWO: THE LIFE OF A LAWSUIT

Notice to the carrier

A lawsuit formally begins with the filing of a petition in court and service of the petition and citation on the defendant physician. As with the notice letter, the physician must immediately notify the carrier upon receipt of service to ensure that an answer can be filed in a timely manner. It is a good idea to contact the carrier by phone first and then immediately forward a copy of the citation and petition. The carrier will then assign a lawyer, if it has not already done so, and forward all material to the lawyer so that an answer can be filed and the defense begun.

Generally in state court, a defendant's answer to a petition must be filed by the Monday following 20 days after service of the citation. If an answer is not filed by this deadline, the plaintiff can obtain a default judgment against the defendant and begin proceedings to execute on the physician's assets for the judgment amount.

Discovery requests may be served along with the petition. This material is also time sensitive, so any discovery must be forwarded immediately to the insurance carrier as well.

Discovery

Once the lawsuit has been filed, the discovery phase begins. During discovery, each party has the opportunity to obtain relevant information and documents from the other parties to the lawsuit. The standard for discovery is broad. Information and documents are properly discoverable if they are "likely to lead to the discovery of admissible evidence," regardless of whether they will be ultimately admissible at trial. Parties and witnesses *must* respond to requests for material that is properly "discoverable."

The physician's investment of time and effort generally begins at this stage. The physician's lawyer has likely already met with the physician to review the events surrounding the claim, the chart, and any other pertinent medical records. During discovery, however, the physician will likely be required to devote some time providing answers to written discovery and gathering any relevant documents requested.

Preparing to give a deposition will require the physician's undivided focus. Beforehand, the physician's lawyer will meet with the physician again to thoroughly prepare for it. The deposition itself could take several hours, and providing the testimony will require a great deal of concentration and focus.

Discovery takes the following forms:

- *Interrogatories* are written questions served by one party on another party.
- *Requests for disclosure* are statutorily predetermined requests for information that must be produced without objection. Disclosures cover the basic information involved in a lawsuit, including potential witnesses, experts, and contentions of the parties, damages, and the identity of healthcare providers who rendered medical care to the plaintiff.
- *Requests for production* are requests for written documentation.
- *Requests for admissions* require the party served to either "admit" or "deny" certain facts and contentions. These requests are particularly time sensitive; failure to respond in a timely manner can result in the admissions being deemed against the party served. The parties must exchange expert reports containing the expert's opinion and basis for the opinion.
- *Depositions* are question-and-answer sessions in which witnesses provide sworn testimony. They usually take place after the completion of all written discovery; the parties are generally deposed first, then the experts.

Primary defenses

Failure of an expert: To maintain a medical malpractice action, a plaintiff must present a qualified expert witness to testify that the physician was negligent and that the physician's actions were the proximate cause of the plaintiff's alleged injuries. *Negligence* is defined as the failure to use ordinary care — that is, the failure to do what a physician of ordinary prudence would have done in the same or similar circumstances. *Proximate cause* is defined as that cause, which, in a continuous and uninterrupted sequence, produces an event foreseeable by the physician exercising the degree of care, required of him or her.

A properly *qualified* expert must be:

- A physician practicing medicine at the time they provide testimony in the lawsuit or a physician who was practicing medicine at the time of the care and treatment that is the basis of the claim; and
- A physician qualified on the basis of training or experience.

Practicing medicine includes training residents or students at an accredited medical or osteopathic school and serving as a consulting physician. Factors considered in determining whether an expert witness is *qualified* include:

- Whether the expert is board certified in an area relevant to the claim.
- Whether the expert has substantial training or experience in an area relevant to the claim.
- Whether the expert is practicing medicine and rendering medical services relevant to the claim.

The physician's attorney can challenge an expert's qualifications and their ability to legally establish "negligence" and "proximate cause." However, if the plaintiff's expert succeeds, a defendant physician must then present a qualified expert to contradict the testimony of the plaintiff's expert. Often, an outside expert is retained, but a defendant physician can be used as an expert on his or her own behalf.

Statute of limitations

Medical malpractice claims have a two-year statute of limitations, which is the time period within which a plaintiff must file a lawsuit. Generally, the two-year period begins from the date of the treatment in question. However, three situations can adjust this strict two-year rule:

- *Notice letter.* Sending a notice letter extends the two-year period for 75 days.
- *Minor plaintiff.* The two-year statute of limitations is "tolled" until a minor plaintiff is 18 years old. Therefore, a viable claim is alive until the minor turns 20. However, parents must file claims for reimbursement of medical bills for treatment rendered while a minor within two years from the date of treatment.
- *Failure to discover the basis of the lawsuit: the "discovery rule."* When a plaintiff is unable to discover the basis of the lawsuit, investigate it, and file a lawsuit within two years of the date of treatment, the plaintiff can file suit within a "reasonable time" after discovering the basis of the suit. For instance, if a patient does not discover that a surgical instrument was retained until three years after the surgery, there are state constitutions that deem the statute of limitations unconstitutional if it precludes the patient from bringing the lawsuit before the basis of it could be discovered.

Mediation

Typically, at some point during the discovery process and before a trial takes place, the court will order the case to mediation in an effort to settle it. However, the parties can also agree to mediate the case without a court order.

Mediation is a nonbinding process in which an independent third party, the mediator, acts to facilitate settlement of the lawsuit. The mediator does not have independent adjudicatory power; that is, the mediator does not listen to both sides of the story and impose a settlement on the parties. Rather, the mediator can only attempt to persuade the parties to reach a resolution. Information disclosed during mediation, if not otherwise admissible, does not become admissible at a trial solely by virtue of its having been disclosed.

Typically, mediation takes a half or full day and requires the attendance of all parties and lawyers, the mediator, and an insurance representative having authority to settle. If the case is not resolved in mediation, the mediator reports to the court only that the parties were unable to reach a settlement.

Pre-trial modes of disposition

Typically, if a lawsuit is resolved before trial, the resolution is accomplished by one of the following methods:

- *Motion for summary judgment*: A motion for summary judgment is a dispositive motion and, if granted, constitutes a judgment on the merits. This motion is typically filed to assert the defense of limitations or to test the plaintiff's ability to produce a qualified expert able to establish negligence and proximate cause.
- *Motion to dismiss*: A motion to dismiss is also a dispositive motion. It is typically filed when a plaintiff fails to produce a curriculum vitae and a qualified expert report establishing negligence and proximate cause within the 180-day period required by statute. Although the statute does allow the court to provide a plaintiff with additional time to comply with this provision, at some point, the plaintiff must produce an expert report and curriculum vitae in order to survive this motion.
- *Voluntary nonsuit*: From time to time, though it is rare, a plaintiff may decide to drop the claim against the physician. This is usually a strategic decision made in a multi-party case when a plaintiff's attorney must choose the theory of the case and narrow the field of medical providers to pursue. This is not a dismissal on the merits, and a claim voluntarily dismissed can be successfully refiled if the statute of limitations period has not expired.
- *Settlement*: Parties settling a lawsuit will typically execute a compromise settlement agreement setting forth the terms of settlement. It can include language stating that the physician does not admit negligence and that the settlement is made only to avoid the time and harassment of defending a lawsuit. The parties will also execute an agreed motion for non-suit to be filed in court. To formally dispose of the case, the judge executes an order of nonsuit in response to the agreed motion.

PERIOD THREE: THE TRIAL

A lawsuit trial is an extremely demanding undertaking, not only on the part of the lawyer, but also on the part of the physician. It can be emotionally, physically, and psychologically exhausting, often requiring the physician's complete and undivided attention to the exclusion of all else.

The trial setting

It may take several years after a lawsuit is filed before it actually goes to trial. A lawsuit filed in state district court can typically take one to three years.

Preparing for trial can be frustrating because a trial date often cannot be firmly established. Generally, the parties to a lawsuit will not know for certain whether they are going to trial until the day of trial, and "special settings," which attempt to set a firm trial date in advance, can also fail. Nonetheless, when trial on a given date is possible but uncertain, both the physician and the lawyer must adequately prepare.

The physician's role

Before trial, the physician must prepare to provide trial testimony, usually by extensively reviewing in depth the medical records, the physician's own deposition, and the depositions of other experts and any plaintiffs. Before trial, the physician will meet with counsel to prepare for direct testimony and anticipated cross-examination questions. Presentation of trial testimony requires complete focus and concentration.

It is best that the physician be present at the counsel table during the entire trial. This means a substantial cut into the physician's practice, perhaps one to two weeks. In addition, it can be difficult for physicians to sit through constant testimony criticizing their actions, qualifications, and knowledge. Even when the testimony is finally finished, relinquishing control over the outcome of the case to a jury of strangers is very stressful; waiting for their decision is appropriately termed "sweating a jury."

TAKE-HOME POINTS

Knowledge is power. This information should prepare physicians in advance so that they can respond appropriately to a claim. While most lawsuits are resolved before trial, a few do warrant a full-blown trial and so require an additional block of time and attention from the physician.

When legal claims arise, the best way for physicians to help themselves is to involve their carrier immediately, be open with their lawyer, be compliant, be available, and be ready to devote some time and effort. To keep peace of mind, however, physicians should rely on their legal team to manage the defense so that they can continue to live life and practice medicine.

These are important concepts of medical malpractice litigation process to understand before you review the behaviors of many physicians practicing medicine. The majority of physicians practicing medicine will have a medical malpractice claim in their practice life. Consider that 18% of claims arise from failure to treat or delayed treatment; 26% of claims arise from a poor outcome or disease progression; 29% of claims arise from complications of treatment or surgery; and 32% of claims arise from a failure to diagnose or delayed diagnosis.

Medical malpractice consumes lots of resources including money, time, and energy. A medical malpractice claim of negligence can be personally devastating and often alters the way physicians view patients and how they practice medicine.

This knowledge and understanding is foundational as you traverse the next chapter, which uses the field of cardiology to highlight aberrant practice patterns that may result in civil and criminal malpractice claims. This awareness will help you assess your approach to the practice of medicine and hopefully help you develop practice patterns that are always within the standard of care.

CHAPTER 14

Clinical Cardiology Practice Patterns

The foundation of clinical cardiology care is a detailed history and physical examination, which allows for a patient-physician relationship to develop and for the cardiologist to develop a differential diagnosis that attempts to identify the etiology of the patient's symptoms and physical examination findings. Despite advancements in technology, the comprehensive history and physical examination are the staples of clinical practice cardiology.

Observations:

- Routine ordering of echocardiography, Holter monitoring, and stress testing prior to cardiac consultation. This results in unnecessary testing and circumstances in which a patient arrives in a wheelchair for a walking/running exercise stress test.
- Routine ordering of blood cholesterol and CT coronary artery calcium scoring in a patient with a low pre-test probability of disease. This often targets low risks groups through advertising and social media.
- Routine echocardiography in patients without symptoms or physical examination findings suggesting significant heart disease. Often the order was for murmur, but review of the medical record revealed no documented heart murmur.
- The large number of ordered tests resulted in review of these tests with patients over the telephone with a non-medical provider to save physician's time.

Consider again:

Waste is defined as using or expanding resources, carelessly to no purpose. In the healthcare arena, waste is manifest when a physician uses resources without purpose, or fails to control costs, and then passes those fees on to CMS for payment. Waste is generally not considered intentional (but it can be). However, overbilling CMS still carries consequences. Examples of waste that are prevalent in medical practice include providing medical services that are not medically necessary and performing tests and procedures that are not clinically congruent with the prevailing standard of care.

Abuse includes intentional, or unintentional practices that directly or indirectly result in unnecessary costs to CMS. Examples of abuse include charging in excess for services or supplies providing unnecessary services that do not comport with the prevailing standard of care, and miscoding on a claim.

This next section gives a detailed outline of the guidelines and evidence supporting cardiovascular testing and allows the reader to perceive the degree of waste, abuse, and fraud being committed in the daily practice of cardiovascular medicine.

CARDIAC CATHETERIZATION

Cardiac catheterization: Cardiac catheterization is a procedure in which a thin, flexible tube (catheter) is **guided through a blood vessel to the heart** to diagnose or treat certain heart conditions, such as arteries filled with plaque.

The coronary angiogram is an excellent test for the diagnosis of coronary artery disease. The use of coronary angiography is indicated when there is a moderate to high pre-test probability of coronary artery disease.

ECHOCARDIOGRAPHY

The echocardiogram identifies:

- The size and shape of your heart, and the size, thickness, and movement of your heart's walls.
- How your heart moves.
- The heart's pumping strength.
- If the heart valves are working correctly.
- If blood is leaking backwards through your heart valves (regurgitation).
- If the heart valves are too narrow (stenosis).

- If there is a tumor or infectious growth around your heart valves.

The test also will help your doctor find out if there are:

- Problems with the outer lining of your heart (the pericardium).
- Problems with the large blood vessels that enter and leave the heart.
- Blood clots in the chambers of your heart.
- Abnormal holes between the chambers of the heart.
- Regional wall motion abnormalities suggesting coronary artery or cardiomyopathy

INDICATIONS FOR ECHOCARDIOGRAPHY IN THE EVALUATION OF HEART MURMURS

Class 1

1. A murmur in a patient with cardiorespiratory symptoms.
2. A murmur in an asymptomatic patient if the clinical features indicate a moderate probability that the murmur is reflective of structural heart disease

Class 11a

A murmur in an asymptomatic patient in whom there is a low probability of heart disease, but in whom the diagnosis of heart disease cannot be reasonably excluded.

Class 3

In an adult, an asymptomatic murmur that has been identified by an experienced observer as functional or innocent.

INDICATIONS FOR ECHOCARDIOGRAPHY IN VALVULAR STENOSIS

Class 1

1. Diagnosis; assessment of hemodynamic severity of the valve disease.
2. Assessment of left ventricular (LV) and right ventricular (RV) size, function, and/or hemodynamics.
3. Reevaluation of patients with known valvular stenosis with changing symptoms or signs.

4. Assessment of changes in hemodynamic severity and ventricular compensation in patients with known valvular stenosis during pregnancy.
5. Reevaluation of asymptomatic patients with severe stenosis.

Class 11a

1. Assessment of the hemodynamic significance of mild to moderate valvular stenosis by stress Doppler echocardiography.
2. Reevaluation of patients with mild to moderate aortic stenosis with LV dysfunction or hypertrophy even without clinical symptoms.
3. Reevaluation of patients with mild to moderate aortic valvular stenosis with stable signs and symptoms.

Class 3

1. Routine reevaluation of asymptomatic adult patients with mild aortic stenosis having stable physical signs and normal LV size and function.
2. Routine reevaluation of asymptomatic patients with mild to moderate mitral stenosis and stable physical signs.
3. Asymptomatic patients without a murmur

OBSERVATIONS IN PRIVATE PRACTICE:

- Stress testing was universally performed in young patients with atypical symptoms or palpitations who had a very low pretest probability of disease.
- Stress testing was frequently ordered by primary healthcare providers with no understanding of Bayes theorem or prevalence of disease.
- Stress testing was ordered on patients with no cardiovascular symptoms but the order sheet would state chest pain and/or shortness of breath. The patient when asked would deny any symptoms.
- There was routine periodic monitoring of asymptomatic patients, after percutaneous transluminal coronary angioplasty (PTCA), or coronary artery bypass grafting, without symptoms or specific indications.
- Routine screening of asymptomatic men and women using exercise testing, with low likelihood of coronary artery disease, was identified.
- Patients having medical conditions classified as severe comorbidity likely to limit life expectancy, and/or candidacy for revascularization.

- Routine nuclear stress testing in patients with normal ECG and low probability of coronary artery disease.
- Routine stress testing in asymptomatic patients with elevated calcium scores and low likelihood of coronary artery disease.
- Widespread use of stress testing on patients with low probability of coronary artery disease and patients who were not candidates for coronary intervention.

ECG TESTING

The standard 12-lead electrocardiogram (ECG) is one of the most commonly used medical studies in the assessment of cardiovascular disease. It is the most important test for interpretation of the cardiac rhythm, detection of myocardial ischemia and infarction, conduction system abnormalities, pre-excitation, long QT syndromes, atrial abnormalities, ventricular hypertrophy, pericarditis, and other conditions.

You may need an ECG if you have any of the following signs and symptoms:

- Chest pain.
- Dizziness, lightheadedness, or confusion.
- Heart palpitations.
- Rapid pulse.
- Shortness of breath.
- Weakness, fatigue, or a decline in ability to exercise.

OBSERVATION IN PRIVATE PRACTICE:

- Routine ECGs in patent without cardiovascular symptoms
- Routine ECGs before the cardiologist met the patient in patients without cardiovascular symptoms
- People not trained in ECG interpretation routinely read ECGs incorrectly.
- Incorrectly-read ECGs led to unnecessary testing and adverse events.
- ECGs were unread for several months, but billed, with evidence of life-threatening ECG changes and the medical record revealing the patient was deceased.

HOLTER MONITORING

Holter monitoring, also known as ambulatory electrocardiographic monitoring (AECG), is considered medically reasonable and necessary for capturing ECG abnormalities in the ambulatory environment. The indications for Holter monitoring may include:

- The patient complains of palpitations and physical examination of standard EKG have not satisfactorily explained the patient's complaints/symptoms. Such symptoms can include but are not limited to chest pain, shortness of breath, skipped beats, palpitations, lightheadedness, or dizziness (syncope).
- The patient has experienced unexplained syncopal episode or the patient has experienced a transient episode of cerebral ischemia which is felt to possibly be secondary to cardiac rhythm disturbance.
- The patient was found to have significant cardiac or conduction disorder and Holter monitoring is necessary as a part of the evaluation and management of the patient.
- The patient has a heart condition associated with high incidence of serious cardiac arrhythmias and/or myocardial ischemia where the Holter monitor is performed as a part of the evaluation and management of the patient.
- The patient has cardiac arrhythmias or other cardiac condition and a cardiac medication that affects the electrical conduction system of the heart has been prescribed with Holter monitoring necessary to evaluate the effect of the cardiac medication on the patient's cardiac rhythm and/or conduction system.
- The patient has a pacemaker and clinical findings (history or physical examination) suggest possible pacemaker malfunction.

OBSERVATIONS IN PRIVATE PRACTICE:

- Recurrent use of Holter monitoring for atypical symptoms or recurrent spells after prior extensive monitoring revealed no arrhythmias.
- There was routine ordering of Holter monitors by primary care and cardiologists prior to the patient being evaluated with a history and physical examination.
- Repeat Holter monitoring when prior monitoring was free of abnormality and no change in symptoms.

HEART FAILURE CLINIC

Heart failure is a complex end result of coronary artery disease, heart muscle disease, hypertension, valve disease, and complex arrhythmias.

Despite the complexity of these heart failure patients, nurse practitioners, and physicians' assistants who were not trained in heart failure cared for the heart failure patients. We cannot expect these unprepared practitioners to provide medical care for these extremely ill patients. This represented another tragedy for the unwitting heart failure patients.

HEART SURGERY

Cardiac surgery is a critical component of healthcare today. Cardiac surgery is often needed to address problems such as heart failure, coronary artery disease, often resulting in heart attack or death, defective heart valves, dilated or diseased major blood vessels such as the aorta, and abnormal heart rhythms.

Cardiac surgery in private practice was often below the traditional expected standard of care. The morbidity and mortality observed was below expectations of national standards. Surgical approaches frequently did not follow guidelines of when it was appropriate to intervene for aortic root enlargement or valve defects. Patients were routinely sent for coronary bypass surgery when the patient had coronary anatomy amenable to lesser treatment approaches that were less risky. Post-op recovery and clinical outcomes were suboptimal. Despite recurrent suboptimal outcomes, a blind eye was applied — the Ostrich phenomenon. Although everyone knew the surgical outcomes did not meet standards of care there was a "silence of the lamb" approach. This looking the other way mandates the need for outside surveillance of complex interventions such as heart surgery.

OUTREACH CLINICS

The outreach clinics represented a tragedy in healthcare. The quality across all aspects of cardiology care was markedly inferior. The physician "leadership" completely understood the deficiencies and chose to turn a blind eye to an abyss of negligent medical care. Clinical decision-making, cardiology testing, and interpretation were below even a poor man's standard of care. Despite this being a serious risk to patient care, no measure was taken to remedy the deficiencies. This led to unnecessary duplication of testing and poor patient outcomes.

CARDIOLOGY LEADERSHIP

Leaders are integral to the success of any organization. Two sets of factors are germane to being an effective leader: character traits and emotional intelligence (EI). Character traits that define great and effective leaders in cardiology include passion, perseverance, and compassion; these are vital complements to their ability to organize, categorize, and communicate. In addition, the success of any organization relies heavily on the sense of responsibility and accountability of its leaders.

Emotional intelligence is the ability of an individual to recognize their own feelings as well as those of others and regulate the expression of those feelings according to the situation at hand. An individual with a strong EI can use experience and vision when making decisions without any influence of emotions. Thus, self-awareness and self-management are key factors affecting an individual's ability to lead.

The examples of leaders in cardiology who have excelled in their field and lead their teams to lasting success are examples of outstanding EI. When interviewed about their successful stories, these leaders stated that what differentiated them from their peers was not necessarily scholarly intelligence or class placement, but their firm determination, perseverance, passion, and ability to deal with diverse situations in an emotionally stable manner.

An effective leader is innovative, can think from different perspectives, and constantly incorporates new ideas in their approach to the ever-changing environment. Good leaders are aware of their own strengths and limitations along with those of their team members. Optimizing every team member's skills by establishing clearly defined roles ensures the organization's worth and competitiveness. Above all, champion leaders have been and are able to embrace criticism and suggestions from their peers. They actually seek criticism. If team members are understood and motivated by their leaders, they feel empowered and more invested in achieving the organizational goals.

The unfortunate opposite face of this medal is made of individuals who are focused on professional recognition and personal gain, who tend to indulge in personal achievements at the expense of their team. This attitude has a negative impact on the organization, leading to decreased work commitment and impaired performance of the team.

Vital to the success of the leader–team relationship is the ability to communicate effectively with the team to execute and implement progressive ideas. A team leader with goals aligned with her or his team's goals motivates the entire team to achieve lasting success. Not only do they maintain an open communication with the team but they also encourage efficient communication between team members to improve patient outcomes.

Medical leaders have educated, trained, influenced, and enabled generations of future cardiologists. Perhaps the most notable outcome of the work performed by these leaders is their ability to leave a legacy of younger generations of physicians that continued and expanded their work, clearly demonstrating the importance of mentorship.

In an era of ever-increasing healthcare costs, it is imperative to develop and implement system-of-care guidelines to attain optimal patient outcomes while maximizing resource utilization. To achieve this goal, the continued influx of competent leaders is critically important.

OBSERVATION IN PRIVATE PRACTICE:

There was no evidence of leadership across any aspect of cardiology.

Medical educators have traditionally been silent on issues related to healthcare cost and value. The experience was one where private practice leadership was mute, and actually actively pursuing strategies of excess care at no value, such as coronary artery calcium scoring in young women leading to down-stream income from stress testing and possible even CT angiograms and coronary artery angiograms.

There was a complete absence of understanding value-based healthcare.

The motivation was to take advantage of fee-for-service medicine while it lasts.

There was no understanding of the "tragedy of the commons" despite our overconsumption of healthcare resources now compromising our ability to handle other pressing social needs.

Succinctly stated, there was no leadership pursuing best healthcare and outcomes. Leadership was pursuing strategies that were attempting to achieve the best financial return through unnecessary testing and treatments.

SECTION 5

Conclusions

It's time to face the facts. Our government is going bankrupt paying for runaway healthcare costs, as are many of our top companies and millions of individual American households. It is time to take a radical approach to fixing healthcare in America.

CHAPTER 15

The "Partial" Healthcare Fix

There is a myth that consumers have completely paid for their Medicare benefits because they pay 1.45% of their pretax wages in Medicare payroll taxes, an amount matched by their employer.

Facts: The payroll taxes that go to Social Security do support the entire program, but in the case of Medicare, our payroll taxes fall far short of paying for Medicare expenses. In 2014, nearly $600 billion flowed into Medicare and $613 billion flowed out. Of the $600 billion, how much do you think came from payroll taxes? — 38% of the total came from payroll taxes. That left $373 billion to pay for. There was $80 billion in Medicare premiums. Doing the simple calculus. Uncle Sam was left with a $250 billion bill. This demonstrates Medicare is clearly a financial bargain for US citizens. The back-of-the-envelope arithmetic clearly reveals healthcare costs strongly superseded our societal contribution through payroll taxes. Recognition of this fact is crucial to deciding how we approach the future of a cash deficit-free fall.

The root cause of the Medicare spending growth is the program's fee-for-service structure: Healthcare providers can charge Medicare a fee when they provide Medicare participants a service. One might think that capping the fees would limit total expenditures, but physicians and hospitals can simply change the classifications of services they provide to ones that provide higher fees. Or they schedule more visits, more expensive tests, and procedures. (Unnecessary cardiac catheterizations, echoes, stress tests, Holter monitors, and cardiac devices.) Or, more likely, they do all of the above.

There is every reason to believe Medicare costs will continue to explode and threaten our nation's finances and our children's economic futures. Fee for service remains the predominant payment mechanism for Medicare and is likely to permit benefits growth in excess of per-capita income growth rate in the future. The nation is facing a Medicare billing practice pattern that is not financially sustainable.

The government-induced healthcare-spending spree in conjunction with rising incomes among highly skilled physicians has led to much better and more expensive procedures, treatments, and medications. Insurers have not appropriated these new treatments in a value-based manner, thus limiting the use of these new medical goods and services. Why? They do not want to risk being sued. Health insurers have passed on their costs in terms of higher premiums. Succinctly stated: Fee-for-service medicine is destroying our population's health and healthcare system.

We have covered a broad bandwidth of issues that raise many questions that must be answered to allow us to achieve high-quality, cost-conscious healthcare. The behaviors identified in this book must be corrected to achieve the goal of effective, equitable, and honest healthcare.

One solution requires the development of federal surveillance of all aspects of our healthcare delivery systems. We must mandate moral and exceptional healthcare across all demographics of our society. The compliance issues and peer review processes require outside periodic review to prevent the misuse outlined in this book. This surveillance system is a large undertaking and must follow in the footsteps of unannounced OSHA visits.

We must take the money out of the process of providing healthcare. Fee-for-service medicine based on RVU production is an existential threat to good healthcare, just as methane and carbon are an existential threat to our climate. The first step to achieving a solution is to recognize the problems addressed here. CMS must develop comprehensive surveillance programs to prevent the waste, abuse, and fraud that is breaking the healthcare piggy bank.

Thanks to decades of fiscal profligacy and the ongoing retirement of the baby boomer generation, the United States is trending toward healthcare insolvency and requires critical and immediate fiscal surgery. The single greatest threat to our nation's finances is the government's runaway spending on Medicare and Medicaid. The decades-long explosion in Medicare and Medicaid expenditures reflects real benefit levels that have been rising at a much faster clip than real income per capita. The expansion of the programs to cover ever more medical goods and services, and major growth in enrollments must be monitored to determine real value in health outcomes.

The financial markets have yet to see the fire at the end of this healthcare tunnel, but it is there and burning ever brighter. Unless we immediately and radically change directions, it will be too late. Millions of baby boomers will retire and become accustomed to receiving higher benefits, notwithstanding the economic toll this will place on the economy and on their children and grandchildren. The partial answer as outlined here is eliminating the incentives for private practice physicians to order more and more tests and services to enhance their personal wealth. This will require surveillance systems that strongly penalize those physicians practicing financially illicit practice patterns of waste, abuse, and fraud.

DEFINE ORGANIZATIONAL VALUES.

Integrity is an essential value in leaders and must be reflected in organizational values to effectively act on well-defined ethical aspirations. If you aspire to lead ethically and with high purpose the leaders and organization must take the time to articulate the importance of those resolutions.

Take the time to have an authentic conversation within the leadership to help precisely define what matters to the organizational leadership, and where institutional values and ethics reside. Second, align your senior team, and prepare to be disrupted by financial incentives that are in conflict with ethical values. At some point, pressure to meet shareholder financial expectations will disrupt your aspirations to lead with a higher purpose and values. Finally, don't wait for the whistle-blowers to surface the issues.

CONDUCT A POST-HOC AUTOPSY.

In 2016, Wells Fargo announced that it would pay $185 million to settle a lawsuit filed by federal regulators and the city and county of Los Angeles, admitting that employees had opened as many as 1.5 million accounts without customer authorization over a five-year period. These unethical practices resulted in an immediate drop in the company's stock prices.

Wells Fargo's CEO attributed the banking scandal to "bad apples" at the company who were fired. But former workers spoke out, saying that they were fired despite being "good apples" who had contacted the company's ethics hotline with concerns about fraud and an unhealthy sales culture. Several employees said they were fired after blowing the whistle.

This breach in ethics stands in contrast to the company's then-publicly stated mission statement to "satisfy our customers' financial needs and help them succeed financially." If you're a physician leader who aspires to lead ethically and with high purpose, consider the following policies.

LOOK DEEP WITHIN YOUR HEART AND SOUL.

The path to higher ethical ambition starts with a deep personal reflection about values and purpose in life. Take the time to have an honest conversation with yourself to help identify what matters to you and where your ethics reside.

Write down key decisions you made in your life and then ask yourself what motivated these decisions. What do they say about you? Did you choose a friendly, collaborative, and ethical culture? Take the time to truly identify who you are and what you truly believe.

ALIGN PHYSICIAN LEADERS WITH THE VALUES AND GOALS OF THE ORGANIZATION.

Start a conversation with your senior physician team members and the workforce of the organization. What kind of organization do they want to create? This type of discussion will allow the leaders to test their own advocacy and then lead the team to a consensus statement. It is critical for all involved to identify how they want to be perceived and what legacy will remain.

PREPARE TO BE ETHICALLY JUDGED AND RESPOND WITH THE VALUES AND ETHICS INCULCATED IN THE ORGANIZATIONAL MORAL/ETHICAL FABRIC.

Shareholder expectations will challenge your aspiration to lead with a higher purpose and values. In real life, there is an inevitable gap between what humans espouse and what actually happens. Human self-deception is real. Schedule routine conversations to check on the reality of the organizational morals/ethics and whether they are concordant with the organization's moral/ethical ambitions.

DON'T WAIT FOR THE WHISTLE TO BLOW.

In many healthcare organizations, lower-level employees feel trepidation and fear speaking "truth to power" about discordant purpose and values. This recognition requires an organizational moral and ethics game plan.

The leadership must be willing to monitor business relationships, billing practices, and the ethical and moral behavior of the medical staff. When there are practices that offend the law (federal regulations), norms (fiduciary duties/ethical behaviors), marketplace (patient quality and safety), and architecture (code of ethics) of the organization, the leaders must respond with action. The cognitive conflict is these actions may impact the financial bottom line.

Consider what the senior leaders of Wells Fargo might have learned if they had an organizational plan to determine if their ethical policies were being met. They would have had the chance to change unethical practices, instill pride and commitment to the company by employees and stakeholders, and avoid financial and reputational damage before the whistle was blown. If you aspire to lead ethically and with high purpose, you must consistently have these honest conversations with yourself, your team, and your organization.

Formal physician leadership is necessary for any medical group practice's success because the physicians ultimately are responsible for the core mission, vision, and values of the practice. Physicians understand how business decisions will affect clinical ones and how clinical decisions will affect business ones. It is not unusual for physicians to be persuaded more by a colleague in an administrative role than by a non-physician in a similar one. Likewise, staff often look favorably at physicians with whom they work in ways that help foster the acceptance of new policies and programs.

Leadership is an acquired skill. Some physicians have a dynamic style; others are quiet. Some always think they are right; others question every decision that they make. Every medical practice should benefit from having a physician in a formally recognized leadership role, regardless of the size of the practice or the individual physician's leadership style. The critical issue is to find ethical physician leadership. This should include formalized academic training in leadership with a strong emphasis on ethics.

CHAPTER 16

Parting Thoughts

As a leader, how do you do the hard things that come with taking on the responsibility of leadership, while remaining a good human being? This is an eternal conundrum for all leaders. Most of us think we have to make a difficult, binary choice between being a good person or being a tough, effective leader. This is a false dichotomy. Being human and making hard leadership decisions are not mutually exclusive. In truth, doing hard things is often the most human thing to do.

To foster the right type of leadership approach, it is critical to acknowledge that we are not our job titles; we are human beings, wanting to connect on a human level with other people. Here are four ways to bring more humanity to your leadership.

1. REMEMBER THE GOLDEN RULE.

Compassion, at its root, is a desire to see others happy and a readiness to take action to help it happen. This is basically an expression of the Golden Rule: *Do unto others as you would have others do unto you.*

The Golden Rule is a helpful step for putting wise compassion in action since it requires the consideration of another person's point of view. When we are able to put ourselves in the other person's shoes, we can take a fresh look at a challenging situation. We can take a moment to recognize that we have one view of the situation, but things may, and probably do, look very different from another person's perspective.

Although putting yourself in another person's shoes is good for reflection, it is important to avoid thinking you know what the other person is feeling or experiencing. This is especially true in today's increasingly diverse work environment. We need to balance putting ourselves in someone else's shoes with not assuming we understand their reality, which requires good listening.

2. LISTEN INTENTLY.

We have two ears but only one mouth. This means we can — and should — listen twice as much as we speak. When you truly listen to others, they feel heard and seen, which satisfies one of our primary needs as humans. If you can listen intently with an open mind and a willingness to learn, not only will you become wiser, but you can genuinely help others.

If you have an important conversation coming up, take extra time to prepare. This may mean establishing the right kind of environment so you can be fully present or setting an intention to really hear and feel what the other person wants and feels versus focusing on fixing a problem.

3. ASK YOURSELF, HOW CAN I BE OF BENEFIT?

A Chinese proverb says, "There is no way to compassion; compassion is the way." Asking how you can be of benefit to others, though, is a "way to compassion." Whenever you are about to engage with someone, take a moment to reflect on what might be going on for this person. What is challenging or going well? And then ask yourself: What support might they need to overcome their struggles? What nudge might they need to gain more self-awareness about their blind spots that are creating difficulties? Reflecting on these questions before you meet people will help to create a more human interaction focused on their growth and development.

4. STRETCH PEOPLE TO SEE THEIR POTENTIAL.

We all want to perform and be appreciated. A good leader values who we are today but also challenges us to stretch ourselves and do better to realize more of our true potential. This is not easy. When someone is already doing well, pushing them to do better can be discouraging and demotivating. But leadership is not about trying to please people and make them feel content and at ease. Leadership is about supporting people by shining a light on things they may not want to face. Instead of shying away from these uncomfortable conversations, try to view your role to stretch people as an indication of true care for them.

When we practice compassion by bringing more of our humanity to our leadership, we can create a culture in which others increase their focus on real human connections. As leaders, we should never underestimate the impact we have on people. We have the power to control their livelihood. We have power over the work they do. And we have power over how they feel treated. This is a huge responsibility. This makes it of the utmost importance to do the hard work of leadership in a human way, so that we can be more successful in positively impacting people's work experience, their sense of commitment, and their job performance.

www.ingramcontent.com/pod-product-compliance
Lightning Source LLC
Chambersburg PA
CBHW061330220326

41599CB00026B/5108
* 9 7 8 1 9 6 0 7 6 2 0 5 4 *